THEN AND THERE SERIES
GENERAL EDITOR
MARJORIE REEVES, M.A. PH.D.

Ancient Athens

E. J. SHEPPARD, M.A.

Illustrated from contemporary sources by
ROSEMARY GRIMBLE

LONGMAN

LONGMAN GROUP LIMITED
London

Associated companies, branches and representatives throughout the world

First published 1967
Sixth impression 1977

ISBN 0 582 20406 2

ACKNOWLEDGEMENTS

We are grateful to the following for permission to reproduce copyright material: The University of Chicago Press for material from *The Iliad of Homer* translated by Richmond Lattimore; The Clarendon Press for material from *Plato: Selected Writings* edited by Sir R. W. Livingstone; J. M. Dent & Sons Ltd and E. P. Dutton & Co Inc. for material from *Herodotus' History* translated by George Rawlinson, edited by E. H. Blakeney (Everyman's Library Edition) and *Plays* by Aristophanes: 'The Knights' translated by J. H. Frere (Everyman's Library Edition); Macmillan & Co Ltd for material from *Hellenic History* by G. W. Botsford and C. A. Robinson, and Penguin Books Ltd for material from *Plato: The Symposium* translated by W. Hamilton, *Plato: The Last Days of Socrates* translated by Hugh Tredennick, *Plato: Protagorus and Meno* translated by W. K. C. Guthrie, and *Aeschylus: The Persians* translated by Philip Vellacott.

For permission to reproduce photographs we are grateful to the following: Alinari: pp. 5, 25, 28; American School of Classical Studies at Athens, Agora Excavations: p. 24; Anderson: pp. 7, 77; Department of Antiquities, Ashmolean Museum: p. 64; Barnaby's Picture Library: p. 63; British Museum: pp. 26, 27, 29, 65, 71, 85; Bulloz: p. 75; J. Allan Cash: pp. 32, 101; Mansell Collection: pp. 67, 79; Paul Popper Ltd: pp. 9, 15, 74, 76, 82. The photographs on pp. 31, 34 (photographer Edwin Smith) and p. 72 are reproduced from *Athens, City of the Gods* by Angelo Procopiou by permission of the publishers, Elek Books Ltd. The illustration on p. 81 is reproduced from Botsford and Robinson, *Hellenic History*, 1939 by permission fo the Macmillan Company of New York.

Printed in Hong Kong by
Sheck Wah Tong Printing Press

CONTENTS

TO THE READER

In this book you will find the names of many Greek people and places. You may wonder how to pronounce them, as they are not at all like English names. One of the easiest is Pericles. This is pronounced as though in English it was written like this—'Pe/rick/lees'. Whenever a Greek name has 'es' at the end, you say this as an extra syllable pronounced as 'ees'. So the name of Socrates is pronounced 'So/kra/tees'. Do you notice that, in both Pericles and Socrates, the 'c' is pronounced like a 'k' in English? Actually, the Ancient Greeks did not have a 'c' in their alphabet, as you will see on page 47, and they wrote Pericles with a 'k' like this ΠΕΡΙΚΛΗΣ. Later, the Romans wrote the names of famous Greeks in their own Latin language, using an alphabet very like our own, and the names came to be written as Pericles and Socrates. This is how they are usually spelt in English books now.

1 The Olympic Games

You have all heard of the Olympic Games and you may have watched some of the events of the 1964 Games on television. These, as you know, were held in Tokyo. But do you know why these athletic competitions are called the Olympic Games? When and where did they begin? Perhaps you saw on television the ceremony which opened the 1964 Games when a Japanese runner entered the stadium carrying a lighted torch with which he kindled the flame that burned all through the days of the games. Where did the torch come from? On Friday, 21 August 1964, the torch was kindled, not from a fire nor with a lighter, but from the heat of the sun and this happened at a place called Olympia in Southern Greece, for it was here that the Olympic Games started a very long time ago. The earliest record of a runner winning a race at Olympia is 776 years before the birth of Christ, but probably the games were even older and had already been held here for some years. This first Olympic victor was called Coroebus and he was a cook from the city of Elis, near Olympia. From 776 B.C. until A.D. 396 when the Games were stopped, the Olympic Games were held every four years, as they are today, but always at Olympia (which is marked on the map on p. 2). Today athletes from all over the world compete, but in the ancient games only free-born Greek men could take part.

In the fifth century B.C. Greece was not one country with one government. It was divided up into many little states, each centred round a city. Why was this? One of the chief reasons was the geography of Greece. Look again at the map on page 2. Greece is a very mountainous country and you can see that the coastline is very much cut up with long peninsulas and deep bays and lots of islands. In one place the

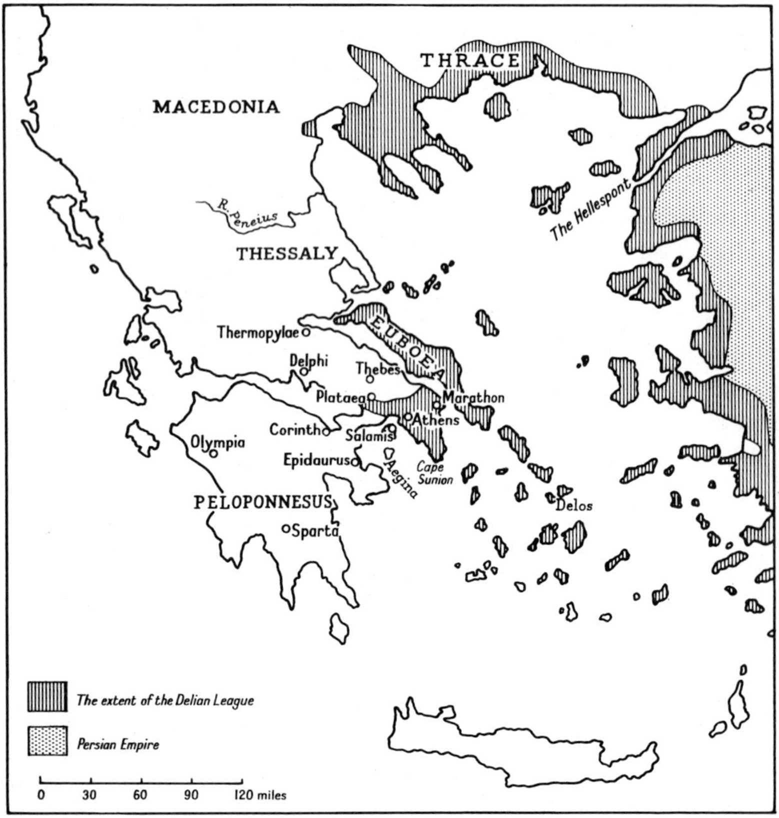

Map of Greece

country is almost cut in two by the sea at the Isthmus of Corinth. So, because of its geography, it is not very easy to travel about from one part of Greece to another, except by sea. Even today this is true, but of course it was much more difficult when there were no motor cars or aeroplanes. The second reason for Greece being divided into many little city states has to do with its history. Many hundreds of years before the fifth century B.C., the country had been invaded by different tribes of Greeks who came from the north, looking for new and fertile lands. They usually settled round a hill which they could fortify and use as a refuge when enemies came. The Greeks called the fortified hill top an *acropolis** and they formed a small city state round it. Sometimes they conquered and occupied an acropolis which had already been fortified by other people, as at Thebes and Athens.

The different Greek tribes spoke different *dialects*. The people of Athens were Ionian Greeks. Their chief rivals were the people of Sparta, who were Dorian Greeks. Can you find these two cities on the map and see how they differ geographically? The southern part of Greece, which is shaped rather like a hanging leaf, is called the Peloponnesus. Sparta is in the Peloponnesus. The Spartans were usually called the Lacedaemonians.

All through their history these two city states, Athens and Sparta, were great rivals and often they fought against each other, as you will read later, but all wars between Greeks had to stop some months before the Olympic Games. The Games were not only an athletic competition; they were part of a great religious festival held in honour of the god Zeus, whom the Greeks worshipped. So, before the Games, three 'truce bearers of Zeus' from his temple at Olympia travelled throughout Greece, proclaiming in every city that fighting must cease. This command was obeyed.

Competitors came from many Greek cities, not only in Greece itself, but also from the islands, and from Asia Minor, for the Greeks were energetic colonists who sailed across the sea to found new cities, just as British and French settlers went to North America in later times. All along the coast of Asia Minor and round the Black Sea there were colonies of Greeks. Cities like Ephesus and Pergamum and Byzantium (now called Istanbul) were founded by Greeks and they also sailed westwards to Sicily and Italy, France and Spain. Syracuse and Reggio, Naples and Marseilles were all Greek colonies. So some of the athletes taking part in the Olympic Games had

* You will find words written like this in the glossary at the end of the book.

quite a long and difficult journey to make. They all had to arrive at Olympia at least a month before the Games started to finish their training under the eyes of the officials.

As the opening day of the Games drew near, crowds began to travel to Olympia, some driving in their chariots, others riding on horseback; some of the rich Greeks from Italy and Sicily even came by boat and were rowed up the River Alpheios in grand barges. Poor folk, the peasants from the Peloponnesus, came on foot bringing wine skins, baskets of fruit and fish and animals for the sacrifices. Outside the sacred area, the plain of Olympia would soon be full of tents and booths with people buying and selling rather like Epsom Downs on Derby Day.

The Festival lasted five days and was held in either August or September according to the year and the moon. On the first day there were sacrifices to the great god Zeus and then the final *scrutiny* of competitors by the officials. In front of a huge statue of the god Zeus, they stood with their fathers and trainers, while a pig was sacrificed, then with uplifted hands the competitors swore that they would use no unfair means to win and that they had strictly obeyed the rules for training in the past ten months. Next the judges or umpires swore to give just decisions. Then the final list of entries was made and the competitors drew lots for heats and ties.

The Games themselves began on the second day with a procession; first came the officials (called Hellanodikai) dressed in purple robes and wearing garlands on their heads, then the herald, trumpeter and other officials, then the competitors, the chariots and the horses and jockeys. As the competitors passed before the spectators the herald proclaimed each man's name, the name of his father and of his city (remember that only freeborn Greeks could compete), and asked if any man had any charge to bring against him. Finally the Games were solemnly declared open and the chariots took their places for the first event. This was a race of about nine miles for four-horse chariots in which they had to make twenty-three turns round the pillars at each end of the course. It must have been a very exciting event to watch, especially when the charioteers tried to turn round the post as fast and as close as possible. Accidents often happened and many dropped out owing to collisions before the long race was completed. It was an expensive business to enter a chariot, almost like running a horse for the Derby today. In the year 416 B.C. a rich Athenian, Alcibiades, entered seven chariots and won first, second and fourth places; after his victory, which he said was for the glory of Athens, he entertained the whole assembly at Olympia at a banquet in a splendid tent he had provided. You can see from the bronze statue found at Delphi how the charioteer was dressed for this race.

The Charioteer

Next came the jockeys' race which was only a single lap; they rode without saddle or stirrups. In the northern plains of Greece called Thessaly they used to breed very fine race-horses. There were also schools for teaching boys to ride, just as there are today. On the next page is a picture of a young man in a riding school, painted on the inside of a cup. What do you notice about his clothes? What is he holding in his right hand?

The third event of the day was the *pentathlon*. This was and

A young man learning to ride

still is today a test for the all-round athlete consisting of five events (*pente* is the Greek word for five and *athlos* means a contest). Do you know what are the five events of the pentathlon today? In the ancient Olympic Games the five events were running, long jump, hurling the *diskos*, throwing the javelin, and wrestling. These were all, except the foot race, performed rhythmically to music played on the flute. The length of the running track was about 200 yards, called a *stade* in Greek, and the race was run on a sandy track enclosed by banks for spectators to sit on. This area was therefore called The Stadium and if you go to Olympia today you can still see the stone starting line in the stadium, sunk into the earth with holes for the posts which divided the base line into sections. Between the posts there were pairs of grooves in which the runners placed their feet. The athletes used jumping weights for the long jump, made either of lead or stone (called *halteres*).

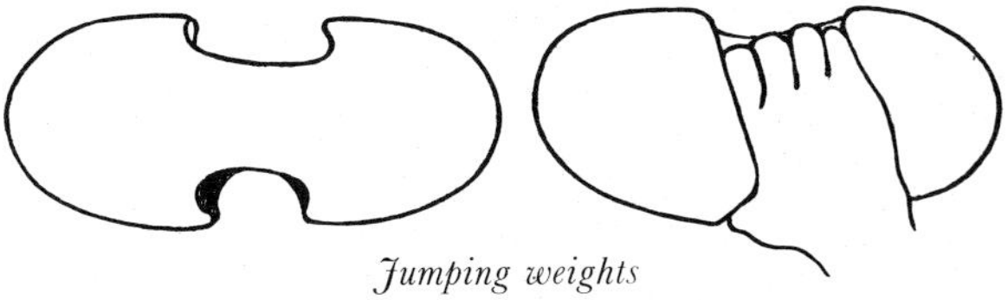

Jumping weights

This one was found at Olympia; it is 11½ inches long and weighs just over 10 pounds. The disc (diskos in Greek) was made of bronze and the aim was to throw it as far as possible. This was one of the oldest and most popular sports in Greece. Below is a picture of a famous bronze statue of the disk-thrower (the Diskobolus); this is a copy of the original one which was made about 450 B.C.

The disk-thrower

On the third day of the Games, the day of the full moon, the men had a rest, for there was a procession and sacrifices on the altar of Zeus, followed by competitions for boys in running, wrestling and boxing. On the fourth day there were more foot races, wrestling for the men and finally the all-in wrestling (called *pankration*) and a race in armour. This was, of course, a military exercise in preparation for warfare. The competitors wore helmets and carried round shields and the length of the course was two stades. The last day of the festival was spent in feasting and rejoicing. The victors received, not gold medals, but crowns of wild olive cut from the trees growing in the sacred grove. In the evening they were entertained at a banquet and when each returned home to his own city he was escorted by friends and brought home in triumph with singing and dancing. All his fellow citizens would go out to meet him, for he had brought honour to their city and in their own temple he would dedicate his crown of victory. Poems were composed and recited in his honour and his name was carved on a stone pillar in his city; he might even have his statue set up at Olympia with a record of his exploits.

You may wonder why the Ancient Greeks were so enthusiastic about athletics. Of course they enjoyed the festivals, but the chief reason for the importance of physical contests was the need for all Greek men to be fit and ready to defend their city against enemies. The contests of skill and strength were a preparation for warfare. The little city states of Ancient Greece were very quarrelsome and so there was often fighting between them, especially between Athens and Sparta, but the Greeks also feared the mighty power of the Persian Empire, whose ruler had conquered Asia Minor and threatened to overrun all the Greek states.

The struggle between the Greeks and the Persians went on for many years and we know a great deal about it, because a Greek named Herodotus wrote a book about it. This is how he begins his history: 'These are the researches of Herodotus of Halicarnassus which he publishes, in the hope of thereby preserving from decay the remembrance of what men have done, of preventing the great and wonderful actions of the Greeks and the Barbarians from being forgotten and especially to put on record the cause of the struggle between them.' Do you notice what he calls the Persians? What does this tell you about Herodotus? He was born at Halicarnassus, a Dorian colony in Asia Minor and lived there for about thirty-seven years, but he travelled far, in order to see for himself many things which he wrote about and to talk to those who remembered and took part in the great war. We know he went to Babylon and Egypt and he recorded many interesting details about the cities and temples there, as well as the customs of the people. His book also contains many good stories. When it was completed, he read it aloud publicly both at the Olympic Games Festival and at Athens.

Entrance to the stadium at Olympia

2 Athens and the Great War against Persia

Herodotus came to live in Athens about the year 447 B.C. Two years earlier peace had been declared between the Greeks and Persians; the Greeks had won their freedom in the long struggle against the Great King of the Medes and Persians. How was it that the tiny Greek states, divided and quarrelling amongst themselves most of the time, managed to defeat the mighty Persian Empire? Herodotus has no doubt about the answer to this question. This is what he says:

> 'Had the Athenians, from fear of the approaching danger, quitted their country, or had they without quitting it submitted to the power of Xerxes [the Persian Emperor], there would certainly have been no attempt to resist the Persians by sea; in which case the course of events by land would have been the following. Though the Peloponnesians might have built ever so many defensive walls across the Isthmus, yet their allies would have fallen off from the Lacedaemonians [the Spartans], not by voluntary desertion, but because town after town must have been taken by the fleet of the Barbarians; and so the Lacedaemonians would at last have stood alone, and standing alone, would have displayed prodigies of valour and died nobly. If then a man should now say that the Athenians were the saviours of Greece, he would not exceed the truth. For they truly held the scales; and whichever side they took must have carried the day. They too it was who, when they had determined to maintain the freedom of Greece, roused up that part of the Greek nation which had not gone over to the Medes and Persians; and so, next to the gods, they

repulsed the invader. Even the terrible *oracles* which reached them from Delphi, and struck fear into their hearts, failed to persuade them to fly from Greece. They had the courage to remain faithful to their land, and await the coming of the foe.'

Have you been able to understand what Herodotus is saying in what you have just read? He says that if the Athenians had run away from their city and given up hope of resisting the Persians at sea, then the enemy would have been able to capture the Greek cities one by one, using their fleet as a base. So the Spartans, whose city was in the south, would have been left alone to fight the invader and, though they would have died bravely, they would certainly have been defeated in the end. So Herodotus says that the Athenians saved the freedom of the Greeks.

Certainly the two most decisive battles in the great war were won by the courage and intelligence of the Athenians, one on land and the other at sea. The first was the famous battle of Marathon. In the summer of 490 B.C. the Persian fleet sailed across the Aegean Sea to attack the Greek cities of Eretria and Athens. They were to be punished for helping the Ionian cities of Asia Minor in their revolt against the Great King Darius. After a siege of six days Eretria was betrayed by two of her citizens; the city was sacked and all the people were made prisoners and sent as slaves to Persia. Nearly every other Greek city north of the Isthmus of Corinth submitted to Persia.

An Athenian citizen arming for battle helped by his wife, who pours the parting cup of wine

The Athenians knew their peril, but they were determined to resist. Herodotus tells us what happened:

'And first, before they left the city, the generals sent off to Sparta a herald, one Phidippides, who was by birth an Athenian, and by profession and practice a trained runner. This man, according to the account which he gave to the Athenians on his return, when he was near Mount Parthenium, above Tegea, fell in with the god Pan, who called him by his name, and bade him ask the Athenians "wherefore they neglected him so entirely when he was kindly disposed towards them, and had often helped them in times past, and would do so again in time to come?" The Athenians, entirely believing in the truth of this report, as soon as their affairs were once more in good order, set up a temple to Pan under the Acropolis, and in return for the message which I have recorded, established in his honour yearly sacrifices and a torch race.

'On the occasion of which we speak, when Phidippides was sent by the Athenian generals, and, according to his own account, saw Pan on his journey, he reached Sparta on the very next day after leaving the city of Athens. Upon his arrival he went before the rulers, and said to them—"Men of Lacedaemon, the Athenians beseech you to hasten to their aid, and not allow a most ancient city of the Greeks to be enslaved by the Barbarians. Eretria, even now, is already carried away captive; and Greece weakened by the loss of one famous city."

Thus did Phidippides deliver the message committed to him. And the Spartans wished to help the Athenians, but were unable to give them any help at once as they did not like to break their established law. It was then the ninth day of the month; and they could not march out of Sparta on the ninth, when the moon had not reached the full. So they waited for the full moon.'

No other Greeks came to help Athens except from the little city of Plataea. The Persian general had landed his troops in the plain of Marathon on the coast northeast of Athens (this is marked on the map on p. 2), for he had been guided by an old enemy of Athenian freedom, the tyrant Hippias.

> 'The Athenian generals were divided in their opinions; and some advised not to risk a battle, because they were too few to engage such a host as that of the Medes, while others were for fighting at once; and among these last was Miltiades.'

Fortunately for Athens, Miltiades knew all about the Persian way of fighting, but he was only one of the ten generals, and the Commander-in-Chief was called Callimachus. So Miltiades went to him and said:

> 'With thee it rests, Callimachus either to bring Athens to slavery, or, by securing her freedom. to leave behind thee to all future generations a memory beyond even Harmodius and Aristogeiton [two Athenian heroes]. For never since the time that the Athenians became a people were they in so great a danger as now. If they bow their necks beneath the yoke of the Medes, the woes which they will have to suffer when given into the power of Hippias are already determined on; if, on the other hand, they fight and overcome, Athens may rise to be the very first city in Greece.'

So Miltiades persuaded Callimachus that the Athenians should risk a battle. Miltiades was confident that they could win it. For several days the armies watched one another. On page 14 is a plan of the plain of Marathon and the two armies encamped. Can you see why the Athenians were in a strong position?

The Medes and Persians had at least twice as many soldiers as the Greeks; most of them were archers. The Athenians relied entirely on their foot soldiers called *hoplites*, armed with a

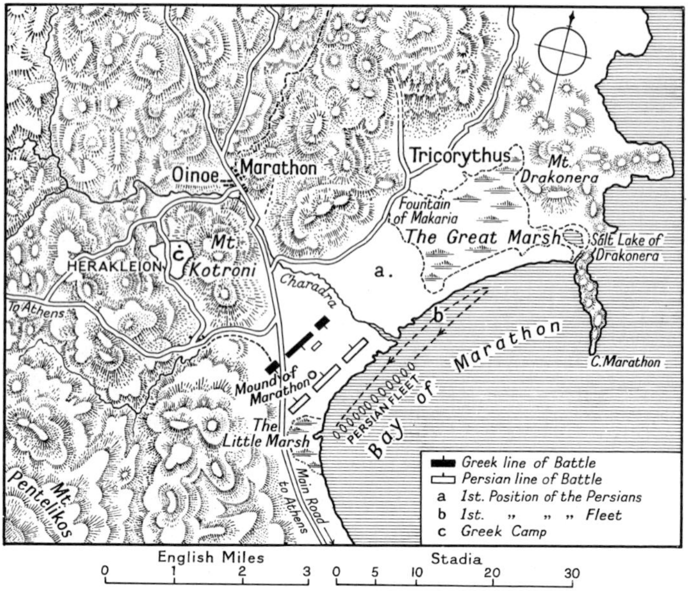

Plan of the Battle of Marathon

short sword and a spear. At last the Persian Commander could wait no longer and advanced across the mountain torrent intending to march south along the main road to Athens. This, of course, Callimachus had already decided to prevent, but the Athenian generals, led by Miltiades, had a clever plan for the battle. They spread out their line thinly in the centre, as their enemies had so many more troops, and relied upon the strong wings to close in as the battle progressed. Not only that, but Miltiades commanded that his men should not move until the Persian arrows began to reach them, then they were to charge at a run. The Persians were not in the least prepared for these tactics nor for hand to hand fighting and very soon their line broke up in disorder and those who could escaped to their ships. According to Herodotus (who, of course, wrote some time after the event) the Persians lost 6,400 men. The Athenian killed numbered 192.

As soon as the battle was over the victors had to set off and march straight back through the hills to Athens, for they knew that the Persian fleet was making for their city. They arrived in time, though the ships were already in the harbour of Phaleron. However, the Persian Commander decided not to risk another battle with the victorious Athenians, so he sailed away. Athens was saved—at least for ten years.

The Mound of Marathon, which was excavated in 1890; it contained 192 bodies with some weapons and funeral vases

The victory of the Athenians at Marathon was hailed with joy by all the Greeks who loved freedom. Herodotus tells us:

> 'After the full moon two thousand Lacedaemonians came to Athens. So eager had they been to arrive in time, that they took but three days to reach Attica from Sparta. They came, however, too late for the battle; yet, as they had a longing to behold the Medes, they continued their march

> to Marathon and there viewed the slain. Then, after giving the Athenians all praise for their achievement, they departed and returned home.'

Before Marathon the Greeks thought it was impossible to defeat the Medes and Persians; now they had been defeated by a small Greek army. The joy and pride of the people of Athens knew no bounds, but they all realized that the war was not over yet. The Great King would not allow his defeat to go unrevenged and Athens must expect another attack. She must prepare her defences. Within the city there were many parties and leaders with different ideas, but one man called Themistocles was certain that he knew how to defeat a second Persian attack. He realized that the huge Persian army could not exist for long without the support of their fleet to bring provisions and supplies and provide transport. So he urged the Athenians to build ships and defeat the enemy at sea before they could attack Athens herself. He was very popular with the ordinary folk of Athens and after a struggle with his enemies, the old noble families, he persuaded the citizens in their Assembly to vote for 200 ships to be built. This navy was to be paid for out of the rich vein of silver which had just been tapped in the mines at Laurium.

Athens had a breathing space in which to build her navy, because Egypt revolted against the Great King, and then Darius himself died. He was succeeded by his son Xerxes, who soon began to gather a huge army for the conquest of Greece. His engineers and workmen were sent to build a bridge of boats across the Hellespont. Herodotus tells us:

> 'Towards this tongue of land then the men to whom the business was assigned, carried out a double bridge from Abydos; and while the Phoenicians constructed one line with cables of white flax, the Egyptians in the other used ropes made of papyrus. Now it is seven furlongs across from Abydos to the opposite coast. When, therefore, the

channel had been bridged successfully, it happened that a great storm arising broke the whole work to pieces, and destroyed all that had been done.

'So when Xerxes heard of it he was full of wrath, and straightaway gave orders that the Hellespont should receive three hundred lashes, and that a pair of fetters should be cast into it. Nay, I have even heard it said, that he bade the branders take their irons and therewith brand the Hellespont. It is certain that he commanded those who scourged the waters to utter, as they lashed them, these barbarian and wicked words: "Thou bitter water, thy lord lays on thee this punishment because thou hast wronged him without a cause, having suffered no evil at his hands. Verily King Xerxes will cross thee, whether thou wilt or no. Well dost thou deserve that no man should honour thee with sacrifice; for thou art of a truth a treacherous and unsavoury river." While the sea was thus punished by his orders, he likewise commanded that the overseers of the work should lose their heads.'

After whipping the sea soundly, the Persians built a second bridge, this time successfully. In the Spring of 480 B.C. Xerxes crossed over it into Thrace at the head of his huge army, and advanced southwards. A plan had been worked out by Athens and Sparta together for the defence of their states. This was to try to defeat the Persian fleet at Artemisium (off Northern Euboea) while 10,000 Greek soldiers under Leonidas, King of Sparta, held the Pass of Thermopylae against the invader. You can read the story more fully on p. 93. The Persians tried for days to force their way through the narrow mountain pass but in vain. Then a traitor led them by a winding track to the rear of the Greeks. Leonidas, knowing they were trapped, dismissed his allies and with his 300 Spartans made a last desperate stand. They were all killed.

The Persian host advanced upon Athens. Themistocles

returned to the city to find the people full of gloom. The *Delphic Oracle* had told them to put their trust in their wooden walls. Some Athenians thought this meant the palisade round the Acropolis, but Themistocles was sure it meant their ships. The Greek fleet had withdrawn from Artemisium, when the Persians had advanced, and now lay in the Bay of Salamis. The Athenians were persuaded to abandon their homes and, taking what possessions they could, the women and children were evacuated to the island of Salamis. Xerxes laid waste the country as he advanced. From Salamis, the Athenians could see their city in flames and scouts reported that the Persian fleet was anchored in the Bay of Phaleron. The courage of the Greeks began to waver, but Themistocles stood firm that they must fight at sea. Meanwhile, he sent off a trusted slave secretly to Xerxes, who was encamped on the shore, saying that the Greeks were panic-stricken and about to sail away and cunningly suggesting that it would be easy to cut off their retreat. The trick worked and during the night the Persian ships sailed into the narrow straits between the island and the mainland of Attica, blocking both exits. The Greeks attacked and the battle went on all day, but by evening the Persian fleet had been defeated and crippled. Their great numbers had only been a hindrance in the narrow straits. You can read an exciting description of the battle, as told by a Persian messenger to the people at home, on p. 96. Once again Athenian brains had defeated Persian might. Their fleet retreated to Asia and Xerxes himself went home to Susa, his capital. Themistocles wanted the fleet to sail at once to the Hellespont and destroy the bridge, thus cutting off Persian supplies, but the Greeks were afraid to risk this, especially the Spartans. So the Persian army was still able to overrun Attica, until the Spartans were persuaded to march north again. Their general won a great victory at Plataea and the Greek fleet sailed across to Asia Minor and won another sea battle there.

Meanwhile the Athenians returned to their ruined city, which must have looked rather like Coventry or Exeter after the air raids in 1942. They were full of energy now and set to work to rebuild the walls of the Acropolis and a strong wall all round the city to make it safe from attack. Themistocles then persuaded them to build dockyards at Piraeus and a massive wall all round the peninsula of Munychia. (These places are marked on the map below.) Can you see why the harbour of Piraeus was better than the Bay of Phaleron for the navy?

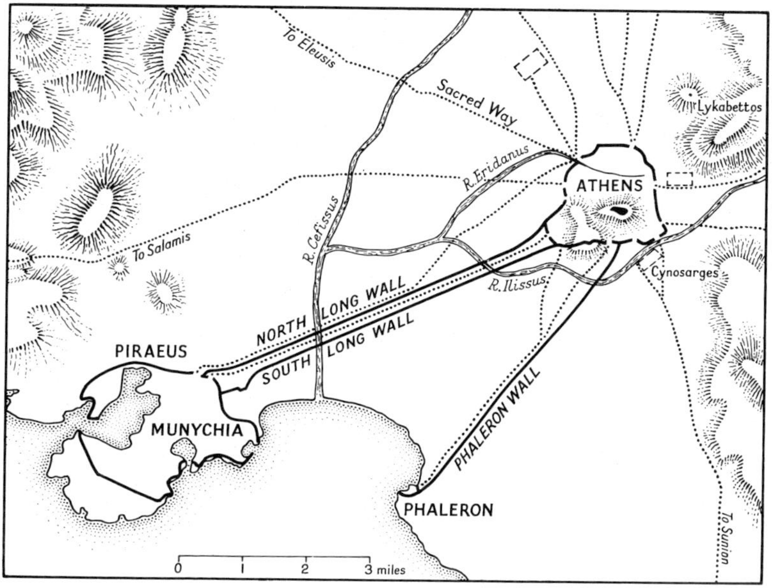

Map showing Athens, Piraeus and Phaleron in the time of Pericles

Most of the Greek city states realised that it was the Athenian navy which had saved them from being conquered by Persia, just as Herodotus says, and so they decided to form a league, with Athens as their leader, to complete the defeat of Persia and protect their freedom in future. Each city made a treaty of alliance with Athens and the sacred island of Delos, where there was a great and holy sanctuary of Apollo, was chosen as the meeting place and treasury of the league. Athens swore that she would protect the other cities and their trade on the sea and would not interfere in their city government. In return her allies agreed to supply either ships or money for the fleet. The big islands like Naxos supplied ships, while smaller states sent money; the amount each should pay was fixed by an Athenian, who did it so fairly that ever afterwards he was called Aristides 'the Just'.

3 Athens After the War

Today people travel from all over the world to see Athens, because of its beautiful buildings and its wonderful history. In the fifth century B.C. her own citizens were immensely proud of their lovely city and called her Athens the violet-crowned. Perhaps this was because of the colours of the great rocky hill in the centre of Athens, their Acropolis or 'high city', which glowed violet and mauve and pink in the sunset light. The Acropolis rises straight up out of the plain, about 500 feet above sea level, with steep cliffs on every side except the west. Standing on the flat top you can see for as far as thirty miles, because the air is so clear and dry. Looking eastwards you can see the great mountains, Hymettos and Pentelikos. Beyond them lies the sparkling Aegean sprinkled with islands like stepping stones. To the north more mountains rise up, hiding the plain of Marathon and guarding the approach to Athens. Only to the south west are there no mountains and here you could see the harbour of Piraeus and across the strait to the island of Salamis. An Athenian could see the whole of his tiny country of Attica as he stood on the Acropolis. Near at hand within the city itself there are other hills but lower than the Acropolis, such as the Pnyx and the Areopagus.

All round Athens there was now a strong wall built for defence, with twelve gates at convenient points. On the north-west side there was a double gate, the Dipylon; the ancient sacred way from Eleusis ran through this and along the north and east sides of the market place to the Acropolis. The Athenians knew that the dangers of further attacks by Persia or by the Spartans were still very real so, at the suggestion of their leader, Pericles, they set to work to build long walls all the way from Athens itself to the harbours of Piraeus. Each wall was 4½ miles in length and they were 550 feet apart. In

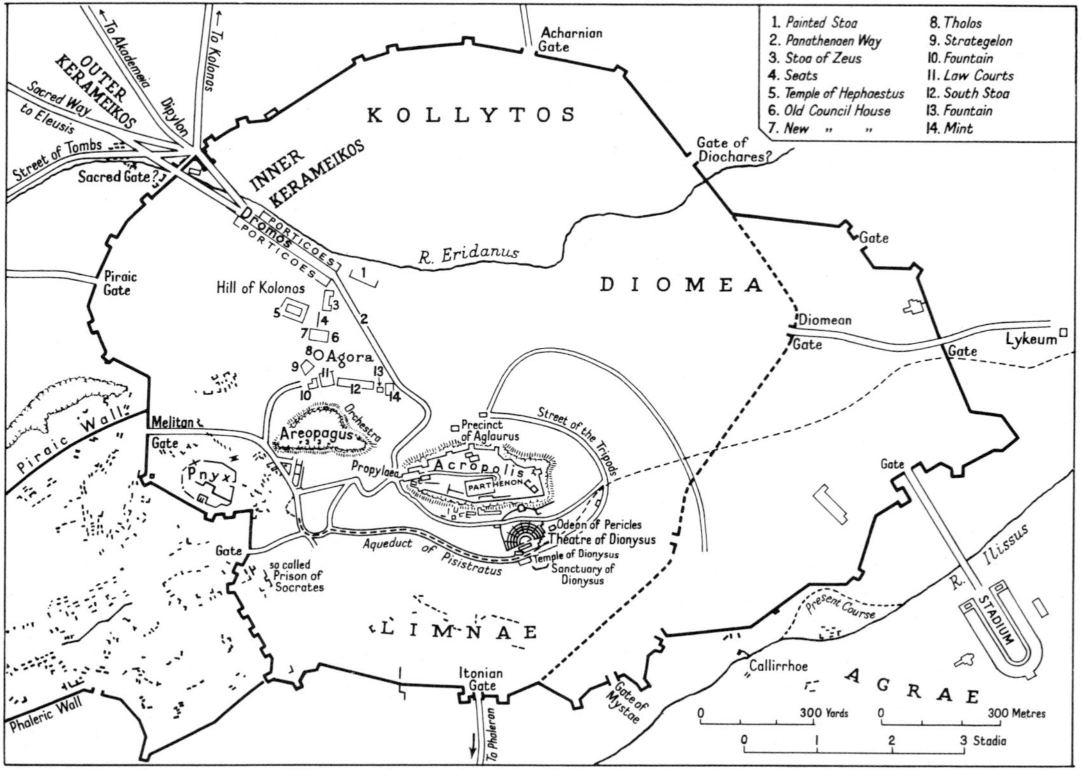

Plan of Athens in the time of Pericles

this way Athens became almost a port and she could never be starved into surrender, as long as she held command of the sea and her harbours. These too were surrounded by a strong wall. The Athenians had suffered so much from the Persians who had burned the farms in Attica as well as looting the city itself that they were determined to make their defences as strong as possible.

Do you remember how the Athenians had to evacuate their women and children and saw their city go up in flames two days before the battle of Salamis? Now that the Persians had been thoroughly defeated and the defences of the city made strong, the Athenians could give all their time and energy to the rebuilding of their temples. They were excited and enthusiastic about this as they loved to make their city beautiful. So they began to make plans first for their Acropolis. Here, in the oldest and most sacred part of Athens, the Persians had done their worst. Even the temple of the goddess Athene, the special protector of Athens, was in ruins. When the walls of the High City had been rebuilt for defence, they had built pillars and bits of the old temple into these walls to tell the story of the Persian attack upon Athens. I wonder if this reminds you of something in England today? You have probably been to see Coventry Cathedral or you have read about it and you know how it was hit by bombs in 1942 during the Second World War. Today you can still see the ruined part to tell the story, but beside the ruins is a glorious new cathedral with lovely stained glass windows. Just as a new and wonderful Coventry Cathedral was rebuilt after the war, so the Athenians decided to build a lovely new temple for the worship of Athene. Their leader Pericles persuaded the citizens to make splendid plans for building the whole of the new temple in white marble. Fortunately, there were quarries not far away at Mt Pentelikos and the marble from these quarries becomes tinted a beautiful golden colour.

The new temple was built beside the old one, on the top of the Acropolis. It took nine years to build. There were two architects called Ictinus and Callicrates who planned the temple, and a famous sculptor called Phidias carved some wonderful scenes for it and also the great statue of the goddess Athene *Parthenos* (which means maiden). So this temple was called the Parthenon. Here is a picture of it as it must have looked when it was finished. Like all Greek temples it appears

A model of the Acropolis and its buildings as they must have looked in the time of Pericles

to be quite simple in design. It was oblong in shape, 230 feet long by 100 feet wide and, as you can see in the picture, the roof was supported on rows of pillars or columns. These, which are the simplest kind of column used in Greek temples, are called Doric. The Athenians felt that simple designs could be very beautiful if all the parts went well together, that is, were in perfect proportion. But though the Parthenon looks magnificently simple, it was really not at all simple to build. The architects knew that if they wanted the lines of the building to look straight they had to make them all slightly curved. This is due to an odd thing we call 'optical illusion', so, though you would never think it, every column in the Parthenon gets narrower towards the top and the lines of the roof and the steps all curve. If you ever go to Athens you can prove this, since if you lie down at one end of the wide steps in front of the Parthenon and try to look straight along the steps to the other end, you will not be able to see it. So the Parthenon shows that the Athenians discovered some real building secrets.

At each end of the Parthenon roof, there was a gable, as you can see in the picture, and for this triangle the sculptor, Phidias, designed and carved scenes from the Greek religion. At the west end, which is the one shown on p. 24, the sculptor showed the great struggle between Athene and Poseidon (the god of the sea) for the lordship of Attica. This contest, so the story said, took place on the Acropolis. Poseidon struck the ground with his *trident* and produced a salt spring, but Athene made the soil bear an olive tree, so she was the victor. This sacred olive tree was always carefully looked after.

Statue of Athene—a copy of the one made for the Parthenon

At one end of the Parthenon was the entrance to the chapel of the goddess and in it stood a huge statue of Athene made of wood covered with gold for her clothing and ivory for the skin. The goddess stood smiling majestically, wearing a golden robe and on her head a great three-crested helmet. In her right hand she held a golden statue of Victory and her left hand rested on her shield. This statue has long since disappeared, but we know what it was like because it was described in detail by those who saw and admired it, and it was also copied in later times.

When the building of the Parthenon was ready, though the sculptures were not yet finished, the Athenians held a great dedication festival; just as there was a special dedication service at Coventry Cathedral, with a procession, so there was in Athens long ago in 438 B.C. You may wonder how we know this, as it is so long ago and there was no television or photography then. The answer is to be found in the sculptured pictures which were carved all round the outside of the Parthenon itself during the next five years. This famous *frieze* was at the top of the building just underneath the roof and so the procession went right round the building, carved in marble, just as it

The Parthenon frieze—Athenian maidens

did in fact on the day of the festival; it was picked out in colours too, red and blue and yellow ochre.

Unfortunately, the Parthenon has been very badly damaged since it was built, chiefly through war; much of the sculptured frieze has been destroyed.

At the head of the procession were the Athenian maidens who had been specially chosen to weave and embroider a new robe (*peplos*) for the statue of the goddess Athene. A man and a boy handed the peplos to the priest and priestess. Next came more girls, some carrying on their heads stools for the gods and goddesses and others with bowls, jugs and a *censer* for the sacrifices. Behind the maidens came the chief citizens and then the animals for the sacrifices, cows and sheep, led by young men. Such a procession needed to be well ordered and so there were marshals to arrange and control it. Here is one of them in the frieze; he is beckoning to those following; these were the foreigners who were allowed to live and work in Athens, but could not take part in governing the city; they carried silver

The Parthenon frieze—a marshal

and bronze trays of cakes to be offered to the gods. Others carried big jars of water on their shoulders. Next came the musicians playing the flute and the *lyre*, which is a small stringed instrument (see picture on p. 48). The musicians were followed by groups of old men bearing olive branches. Then came what must have been the most exciting part of the procession to watch—a cavalcade of four-horse chariots each guided by a charioteer and accompanied by an armed runner. Here the marshals had to control and restrain the procession, for the horses were very high-spirited and used to chariot racing. Finally, bringing up the rear of the procession, came a thundering troop of all the finest young men of Athens, riding on horseback. They did not wear uniform, but were dressed in various ways, some in tunics only, some in cloaks and hats, others in armour. Here is a picture of two of these young riders from the Parthenon frieze.

The Parthenon frieze—young riders

You must imagine for yourselves what this long procession must have looked like as it wound its way through the streets of Athens and then up the steep slope of the Acropolis along the sacred way to the eastern end of the Parthenon. Here the sculptor pictured the gods and goddesses waiting to receive the offerings of the citizens and taking their part in the festival. Here are three of them. As you can see, the Greeks thought of

The Parthenon frieze—three gods

their gods as beings exactly like themselves, only more powerful and beautiful than most human beings. So they brought their presents to the temple of Athene in this great festival.

The goddess as warrior was there too on the Acropolis, for right in the centre, opposite the entrance, the Athenians set up a huge bronze statue of Athene. Only the marble base is there today, but we know from descriptions by those who saw the statue that it was so big that sailors returning to Piraeus could see the sunlight glinting on Athene's spear as they rounded Cape Sunion.

As soon as the Parthenon had been dedicated, Pericles started plans for a grand new gateway to the Acropolis at the western end. The architect planned to build a central gateway with long pillared porches on either side, but he ran into trouble here, because the rock was all sacred ground and the priests opposed him. So only part of this was built; it was called the Propylaea. One small room built on the left of the gateway was a picture gallery.

On the righthand side, where the rock juts out, there was an ancient tower with an altar and sanctuary dedicated to victorious Athene, for the Athenians believed that their goddess was their helper and protector both in peace and war. Pericles decided to build a new temple here and this too was made of marble; it was called the Temple of Athene Nike, meaning victory, and was decorated with a frieze picturing Athenian soldiers fighting against the Persians. Later, when the Athenians were fighting against the Spartans and the war was going badly, they added a small parapet in front of the Temple and decorated it with sculptures of their goddess surrounded by winged victories bringing her shields and helmets. This they believed would help them to win the war. These winged victories, even though today they are badly damaged and headless, still show what beauty the Athenian sculptors could express in stone.

One of the most ancient sanctuaries on the Acropolis was a small one, near the north-west corner, in which there were altars to several Athenian gods and heroes, especially one called Erechtheus. So this sanctuary was called the Erechtheum. Like the other sacred buildings on the Acropolis, it had been destroyed by the Persians, but now Pericles planned to rebuild it. This was done after he died. This new Erechtheum was a rather unusual building, because it had to be

Winged Victory

built on three different levels, as all the ground was too sacred to be levelled. The result was that the architects planned and built a most charming and graceful little temple. It had three porches, two of which were supported on tall Ionic pillars (these are the kind that have curled ram's horns at the top). The third porch on the south side was unique in Greek architecture, because the roof rests on statues of maidens carrying baskets on their heads; they are called *Caryatids*. There are six of them, but one is a copy, because the original one is now in the British Museum. Inside the Erechtheum there lived a sacred serpent, which was fed with sweetmeats; the Athenians believed that it guarded their Acropolis and if it refused the food offered, then disaster would follow for Athens. (See page 101 for a picture of the Caryatids.)

So Pericles' plans made Athens the most beautiful city in Greece which attracted the best artists, craftsmen and thinkers.

The Acropolis as it is today

4 The Athenian Family at Home

Because the weather was usually dry and sunny, the Athenians lived out of doors most of the time, and men especially were rarely at home in the daytime. But of course they came home at night to sleep and sometimes they entertained men friends in their homes. These homes were very simple indeed when compared with our houses today, partly because the Athenians chose to make their city with its temples and public buildings beautiful rather than to spend time and money on their homes. So we know much more about their temples than their houses, especially as remains of these have long ago disappeared, but the foundations of some houses have been excavated. These show that the Athenian's house was small and usually built round an open courtyard so that the rooms opened on to this. The wall of the house along the street usually had no windows, so that curious passers-by could not look in. It was quite private for the family. If a Greek burglar wanted to break into a house he had to dig a hole in the wall, which was made of sun-dried brick, and so the Greek word for burglar was 'wall-digger'. Some of the houses had two storeys, but most were only of one storey. Houses in Athens were, in fact, probably very like those you can see today in Mediterranean villages, whether in Greece or Sicily or Crete. Outside most houses stood a pillar with a bearded head of the god Hermes on the top, guarding the home.

Inside the front door of the house there might be a small porch or cupboard for the porter, who was a slave trusted by his master to guard the family against intruders. You will find a story about the porter on page 57. Athenian men spent most of their day in the city, either at work or leisure; the women, at least those of good families, were not expected to leave their houses or appear in public except for special occasions such as festivals or weddings, and never went out without being attended by a man of their household. So the women mostly stayed at home and managed the house and children. Both boys and girls were brought up by their mothers until they were seven, but then boys went to school while girls were taught at home all that a good wife and mother would need to know.

Mother and baby

The women of the household, the mother and daughters and slave girls, if any, all lived in the most private part of the house, the women's quarter, which was shut off from the courtyard by a door. Beyond this no visitors would dare to go, but when the family were alone they all used the courtyard for meals or play. In the women's part of the house there were bedrooms, storeroom and kitchen. The only permanent fireplace was in the kitchen for cooking. Otherwise in winter a movable *brazier* was used for heating when necessary.

Like the houses, Athenian meals were simple except for a dinner party and even then the conversation and entertainment were considered more important than the food. The first meal of the day was taken very early, as they got up at dawn or very soon after and we should hardly call it a meal at all, for it was only a small piece of bread dipped in wine! This was all they had to eat and drink for breakfast and it had to last them until midday, when they had luncheon. This was a more solid meal of bread, goat's-milk cheese, figs and olives and perhaps some fish; the family ate it together either in the courtyard or under the covered *portico* of the courtyard. I expect you realise that the Athenians had no tea or coffee to drink, so they drank wine mixed with water. Grape vines grow very easily in Attica, so wine was cheap and everyone could afford it. Instead of sugar for sweetening, they used honey. Near Athens there was a mountain called Hymettos which was famous for its purple thyme flowers from which the bees made wonderful honey. Olive oil was also very important for cooking as the Athenians had no butter or margarine or lard. Household shopping was done by the men, who went to the market place, followed by one slave at least, to buy the fish and fruit and olive oil. When a new catch of fish arrived in the market, a bell was rung, so that everyone could come and buy fresh fish.

An Athenian citizen loved to entertain his friends in the evening at a dinner party. He did not send out written invitations beforehand, but as he walked to the market place in the early morning to do his shopping he would invite friends he met to come to dinner that evening or the next. Sometimes one of his guests brought along a friend unexpectedly. If it was a very special occasion, such as a birthday or the naming of a son, then the host would engage a professional cook for the evening. He could arrange this when he went to the market place and he could also hire some flute girls if he wished. As the guests arrived, their host greeted them with a welcoming look and a word of greeting, but he did not shake hands. Then the guests sat down on the couches, which had been arranged ready in the dining room, and a slave took off their sandals or shoes and poured scented water over their feet to remove any dust from walking through the streets. The dining room was lighted by oil lamps; these were made either of pottery or of bronze with a floating wick; the lamp was placed on a stand or sometimes hung by a chain from the ceiling.

The guests reclined on the couches lying on the left side, supported on their left elbows against the cushions. It was a point of good manners to recline gracefully. One of the comic play-writers of the time, called Aristophanes, wrote about a smart son trying to teach his father how to behave like a man of the world at a dinner party. The son says, 'Come and lie down' 'How?', asks the old man. 'Gracefully.' 'Like this?' 'Nothing of the sort.' 'How then?' 'Stretch out your knees and shed yourself in an easy and supple way along the cushions, then praise some article among the bronzeware, gaze at the patterns on the ceiling and admire the curtains of the courtyard.'

In the picture you can see a man reclining, and in front of the couch a slave has placed a low table and then come round with a water jug to pour water over the guests' hands, for they

A guest at a dinner party

had no knives and forks and ate with their fingers. Occasionally they used spoons for shell fish and soft bread was used instead of napkins. The first course at dinner was fish or eels or a quail, but rarely meat. With it they ate vegetables which were cooked in oil or served with sauces or honey. They did not drink any wine with their food. After this a slave brought water again to wash the guests' hands and took away the tables (which must have needed cleaning by this time), and swept the cement floor—there was no carpet—for all remains such as shells or bones had been dropped on the floor! When this was done a flute girl sang; then the host poured out some wine, with the words 'To the god' or 'To good health' and the second part of the banquet began. The tables were brought back for dessert, consisting of salted almonds, fresh or dried figs, grapes or other fruits, sweetmeats, cheese and salt.

These two courses completed the dinner and now came the second part of the banquet, called 'The drinking together' or 'Symposium'. First of all, the host poured out some wine to honour the gods and a slave brought in wreaths or garlands to crown each guest. These were made by the women, of ivy or myrtle twined with wild flowers such as violets, hyacinths, or roses, according to the season. The flowers were picked on the mountains near Athens, especially the great steep one called Lykabettos, and brought in by the poor country women to sell in the market. The flower sellers also made garlands ready for sale. The wine was always mixed with a great deal of water and for this a large jar was needed. On the next page is a drawing of some *vessels* used at a dinner party. Sometimes the son of the house would mix the wine and carry it in a jug to serve the guests. The cups from which they drank were made either of pottery, if the host was poor, or of bronze or silver; they never used wine glasses. The Athenian home had little furniture, but they always had a great many jars, bowls and mixing vessels.

The Athenians thought it was rude and barbarian to drink

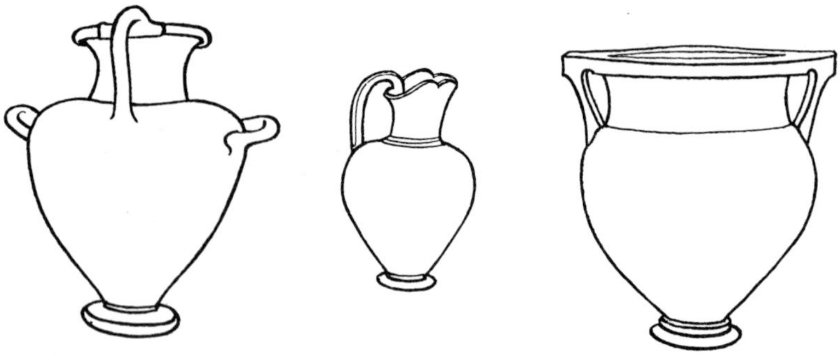

Vessels used at a dinner party

too much. One *comedian* says, 'The first cup means health, the second pleasure, the third is for sleep and then wise men go home. The fourth means rudeness, the fifth shouting, and the sixth disorder in the streets, the seventh black eyes and the eighth a police summons.' Says Aristophanes: 'Drinking is bad; for wine means banging at doors, hitting people and having to pay for it and a headache into the bargain.' And another writes: 'This is the Greek way of drinking, to use moderate-sized cups and chat and talk pleasant nonsense to one another. The other way is swilling, not drinking, and it is deadly.' The 'drinking together' was an excuse for good conversation, singing, watching dancing, or asking riddles. Every educated man was expected to be able to entertain his friends by playing the lyre and singing a lyric poem to it. The lyre was handed round and each one sang in turn. Sometimes, if the host could afford it, there were professional dancing girls or acrobats to entertain the guests, but always the conversation was important.

Here is a story about the famous teacher Socrates going to a dinner party, told by Apollodorus to an unnamed friend.

> 'Aristodemus said that he met Socrates fresh from the bath and sandalled: and as the sight of the sandals was unusual, he asked him where he was going so finely dressed:

"To a banquet at Agathon's," he replied, "whose invitation to his sacrifice of victory I refused yesterday, feeling that there would be a crowd, but promising that I would come today instead: and I have put on my finery because he is a fine man. What say you to going with me unasked?"

'"Yes," I replied, "I will go with you, if you like. But I shall say that I was asked by you, and then you will have to make the excuse."

'"Two going together," he replied, in Homeric fashion, "may invent an excuse by the way".

This was the style of their conversation as they went along on the way. Socrates stayed behind in a fit of abstraction, and desired Aristodemus, who was waiting, to go on before him. When he reached the house of Agathon he found the doors wide open and a comical thing happened. A servant, coming out, met him, and led him at once into the banqueting-hall in which the guests were reclining, for the banquet was about to begin.

'"Welcome, Aristodemus," said Agathon, "you are just in time to dine with us; if you come on any other business put that off and make one of us, as I was looking for you yesterday and meant to have asked you if I could have found you. But what have you done with Socrates?"

'I turned round and saw that Socrates was missing, and I had to explain that he had been with me a moment before, and that I came by his invitation.

'"You were quite right in coming," said Agathon; "but where is he himself?"

'"He was behind me just now, as I entered," he said, "and I cannot think what has become of him."

'"Go and look for him, boy," said Agathon, "and bring him in; and do you, Aristodemus, meanwhile take the place by Eryximachus."

'The servant then assisted him to wash, and he lay down,

and presently another servant came in and said that our friend Socrates had retired into the portico of the neighbouring house. "There he is fixed, and when I call to him," said the servant, "he will not stir."

' "How strange," said Agathon; "then you must call him again, and keep calling him."

"Let him alone," said my friend, "he has a way of stopping anywhere and losing himself without any reason; do not disturb him, as I believe he will soon appear."

' "Well, if you think so, I will leave him," said Agathon. And then, turning to the servants, he added, "Let us have supper without waiting for him. Put on the table whatever you like, as usual when there is no one to give you orders, which I never do. Imagine that you are our hosts, and that I and the company are your guests; and treat us well, and then we shall commend you." After this they had supper, but still no Socrates; and during the meal Agathon several times expressed a wish to send for him, but Aristodemus objected; and at last when the feast was about half over—for the fit, as usual, was not of long duration—Socrates entered. Agathon, who was reclining alone at the end of the table, begged that he would take the place next to him; "that I may touch the sage," he said, "and have the benefit of that wise thought which came into your mind in the portico, and is now in your possession; for I am certain that you would not have come away until you had found what you sought."

' "How I wish," said Socrates, taking his place as he was desired, "that wisdom could be infused by touch, out of the fuller into the emptier man, like water which is poured through wool out of a fuller cup into an emptier one; in that case how much I should prize sitting by you! For you would have filled me full of much and beautiful wisdom, in comparison of which my own is of a very mean and questionable sort, no better than a dream; but yours is bright and only beginning, and was manifested forth in all the splendour of youth the day before yesterday, in the presence of more than thirty thousand Hellenes." [He had won a prize at the Spring Festival for the best serious play].

'"You are mocking, Socrates," said Agathon, "and before long you and I will have to settle who bears off the palm of wisdom—of this Dionysus shall be the judge; but at present you will be better occupied with the banquet."

'Socrates took his place on the couch, and dined with the rest; and then *libations* were offered, and after a hymn had been sung to the god, and there had been the usual ceremonies they were about to begin drinking, when Pausanias said, "And now, my friends, how can we drink with least injury to ourselves?"'

The guests all agreed that they did not wish to drink much wine or listen to the flute girl, but that they wanted to talk and each guest in turn was asked to make a speech in praise of the god of love. One of them was the writer of comic plays, Aristophanes; he made them all laugh. He was followed by Agathon, the host, and Socrates.

'When Socrates had done speaking, the company applauded, and Aristophanes was beginning to say something in answer to the allusion to his own speech which Socrates had made, when suddenly there was a great knocking at the door of the house, as of revellers, and the sound of a flute-girl was heard. Agathon told the attendants to go and see who were the intruders. "If they are friends of ours," he said, "invite them in, but, if not, say that the drinking is over." A little while afterwards they heard the voice of Alcibiades resounding in the court; he was in a great state of intoxication, and kept roaring, and shouting, "Where is Agathon? Lead me to Agathon," and at length, supported by the flute-girl and some of his companions, he found his way to them, "Hail, friends," he said, appearing at the door crowned with a massive garland of ivy and flowers, his head flowing with ribands, "Will you have a very drunken man as a companion of your revels? Or shall I crown Agathon, which was my intention in coming, and go away? For I was unable to come yesterday, and therefore I come today, carrying on my head these ribands, that taking them from my own head, I may crown the head of this fairest and wisest of men, as I may be allowed to call him. Will you laugh at me because I am drunk? Yet I know very well that I am speaking the truth, although you may laugh. But first tell me; if I come in shall we have an understanding? Will you drink with me or not?"'

As you can see, this young man, Alcibiades, was one who did not know when it was time to stop drinking wine and go home to sleep. The story ends with all the guests having fallen asleep by dawn except Socrates and his friend—

'Socrates, when he had laid them to sleep, rose to depart; Aristodemus, as his manner was, following him. At the Lyceum he took a bath, and passed the day as usual. In the evening he retired to rest at his own home.'

A woman spinning

You must have noticed that, except for flute-girls, there were no women at a feast. You may wonder what the women found to do all day as they did not go out shopping or to work, except for some of the poor folk who kept stalls in the market. The picture on page 42 tells you one thing that the women did at home. Now study the next picture of women at home and find out all you can from it, especially about their clothes and hair styles. The one sitting down on the left is

Women at home in Athens

doing embroidery on a frame. In a hot country like Greece, people do not need many clothes, so women usually wore only a light tunic or under-dress in the house. When going out to visit a woman friend or at a festival they wore over this a large drapery which you can see on the lady second from the left in the picture. Both tunic and mantle could be arranged in all sorts of ways. On the next page is a picture of a girl beginning to put on her tunic. Tunics were of all colours, but saffron yellow was a favourite one, and they were decorated with borders and fastened with a brooch on the shoulder and a girdle round the waist. There are girdles hung up in the picture. Hair styles were varied, as you can see, but women dressed their own hair at home. Every Athenian woman longed to have golden

A bridal procession

hair, or else blue-black, so, if you were not fortunate enough to be born with the right colour, you sometimes dyed it. Make-up, too, was used a great deal, and evidently some ladies overdid it, for a comic poet says, 'If you go out in summer, from your eyes there run two streaks of black; from your cheeks perspiration makes a red furrow down your neck; and when your hair touches your neck it gets white with white-lead.'

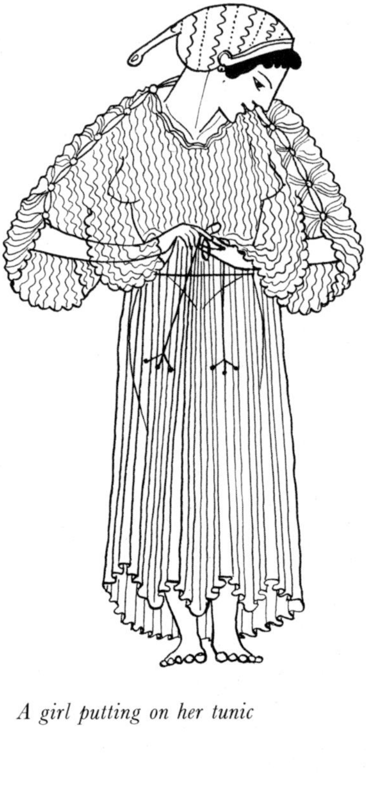

A girl putting on her tunic

Marriages were arranged either by a girl's father or by a woman matchmaker. A girl was married between the ages of fifteen and twenty to a man a good deal older than herself. The girl's father was obliged to produce a *dowry*, but this remained her own property after marriage. So a wealthy wife sometimes bullied her husband! The *betrothal* was a solemn contract between the future bridegroom and the girl's father or male guardian; the girl herself need not be present and had

no say in this—in theory at least! A ceremony of 'pledging' or 'giving away' took place in the home and then later, usually in the winter month called 'Gamelion', came the 'fetching home' when the bride was fetched by her husband after the wedding feast. The wedding cake was made of pounded *sesame* seeds mixed with honey. The bride was veiled, but men and women feasted together for this special occasion. In the evening a flute player was heard at the door; the mother of the bride and also the bridegroom's mother each lighted a pair of torches and then led the bride, still veiled, out to the carriage in which she rode to her new home sitting between the groom and the best man, both wearing wreaths on their heads, and followed by a procession of friends dressed in white singing a special wedding song. The door of her new home was decorated with olive and laurel boughs and confetti was scattered over the couple and the bride ate a piece of *quince* before she was led into the house. Next day the newly wedded couple were at home to their friends and the bride, now unveiled, received the wedding presents. Can you think what kind of presents the visitors would bring?

5 The Athenian Citizen—His Education

An Athenian boy went to school when he was six or seven years old, but you will be amused to learn that the boy walked to school followed by an old and trusted slave who was called a *paidagogos*, which means 'a boy keeper'! This paidagogos was responsible for seeing that the boy did not play truant, that he walked properly and behaved well in the streets; he also carried the boy's *writing tablet* or books or musical instruments to school and stayed there throughout the lessons. He was not supposed to let the boy out of his sight, and was allowed to beat the boy if he was naughty, so he carried a long cane. The first lesson would be learning the letters of the Greek language. The first two letters were called alpha, beta, so you can see where our word 'alphabet' comes from. On the opposite page the Greek alphabet is printed. In the lefthand column are the capital letters used then; the righthand column gives the English sound for the Greek letter as nearly as possible. How many of our letters come from the Greek ones?

In order to make it easier to learn, the alphabet was set to music and sometimes the spelling was acted as a play, with boys representing the letters. When they had learnt their letters, they could begin to learn to read. This was not very easy as there were no spaces between the words and no punctuation. This is what the great Athenian teacher Plato said about learning to read: 'When the boys knew their letters and were beginning to understand what was written, the masters put beside them on the benches the works of good poets for them to read, and made them learn them by heart. They chose stories and praises of the heroes of old in order that the boy might admire them and imitate them.' Homer was the chief poet and all the schoolboys knew his exciting stories of the Trojan War and the adventures of Odysseus. Long passages

The Greek Alphabet

as it was written in Pericles' time	*as it is written today*	*names of the Greek letters*	*The nearest English letters*
A	Α	alpha	A
B	Β	beta	B
Λ	Γ	gamma	G
Δ	Δ	delta	D
E	Ε	epsilon	E (*short*)
I	Ζ	zeta	Z *SD*
H	Η	eta	E (*long*) H
ʘ	Θ	theta	Th
I	Ι	iota	I
K	Κ	kappa	K
L	Λ	lamda	L
M	Μ	mu	M
N	Ν	nu	N
XS or XΣ	Ξ	xi	X *KS*
O	Ο	omicron	O (*short*)
Γ	Π	pi	P
P or R	Ρ	rho	R
Σ or S	Σ	sigma	S
T	Τ	tau	T
V	Υ	upsilon	U
Φ	Φ	phi	Ph, F
X	Χ	khi	Kh, Ch
ΦS or ΦΣ	Ψ	psi	Ps
Ω	Ω	omega	O (*long*)

The alphabet was changing during the 5th century B.C. The three letters eta, xi and omega were not in the official alphabet until 403 B.C.

were learnt by heart and recited and one Greek writer actually learnt the whole of Homer. This is what he wrote: 'My father, wishing me to grow up into a good man, made me learn all the lines of Homer, and now I can repeat the whole of the Iliad and Odyssey from memory.' (This would be about 26,000 lines of poetry!)

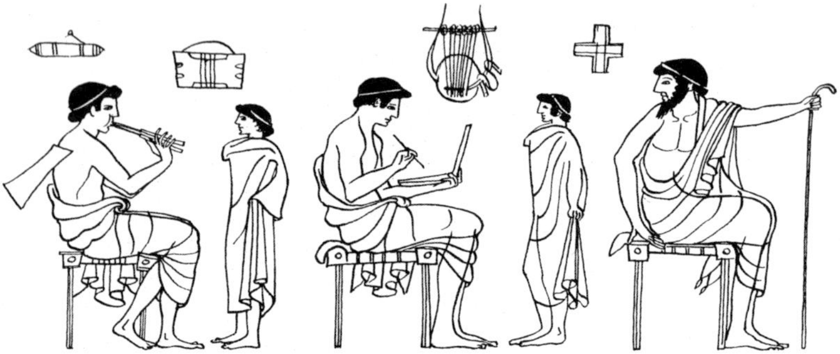

A primary school in Athens

Here is a picture of a primary school which was painted round a big bowl by an Athenian artist. Find out all you can from it about the other kinds of lessons the boy learnt before you read on. Who is the man sitting on the righthand side of the picture? As you can see, the boy stands in front of his teacher and seems to be taught alone, but this may be because the painter could not manage to show a row of boys in the space. In the middle the master is giving a writing lesson; he holds the folded writing tablet open; this was covered inside with wax and writing was done with the pointed *stylus* which the master is holding. Another closed tablet hangs on the wall behind and also a scroll and a ruling square.

You will want to know if the boys learnt to do arithmetic in the primary school. It is not quite certain that they did, but as some boys never went to a secondary school, because their parents could not afford the fees, it is probable that they learnt enough simple arithmetic to be able to buy and sell in the market and do the sums needed for their trade. They may have learnt something about their complicated calendar too, as it was very important to know about the seasons for farming. The year began in our July with the new moon and was divided into twelve months according to the moon. Each month in the year was divided up into three parts of ten days each; these were called 'moon standing up, moon in the middle and moon declining'. As counting was done on the fingers this meant that you could count on both hands for each part of the month.

If you have studied the pictures carefully, you will have found out that boys learnt to play either the lyre or the double flute. Every Athenian man was expected to be able to entertain his friends at a dinner party by singing and playing on the seven-stringed lyre; if he could not, he was thought very uneducated. Music and words went together. Sometimes the boys learnt the laws of Athens set to music. In the next picture of a music class you can find out for yourself some more about going to school in Athens. This one was painted on a big water jar.

A music lesson

We do not know how much the schoolmasters of Athens charged for their teaching, but as even poor boys received some education it seems that fees must have been low. These were paid monthly by the parents and a Greek writer says that the mean man does not send his children to school all the month of Anthesterion (that is, from the middle of February to the middle of March) because of the number of festivals which were all holidays. Of course, there was no weekend holiday then.

Physical education was very important in Athens and the whole of Greece for three reasons; first, because the Athenians loved beautiful bodies, which were healthy and well-developed. The other two reasons you will find in Chapter I of this book. So every Athenian boy started his physical education as soon as he went to school and continued this until he was a man, in a school specially set aside for teaching athletics. First he went to one called a *palaestra*. This was a simple building surrounding an open space with a sandy floor for exercise. The boys were grouped into classes according to age and were taught by a specially trained master called a *paidotribes*, which probably means 'boy rubber'. (You will discover further on what he rubbed the boy with and why.) When the boy arrived, followed of course by his paidagogos, he would go into the undressing room and strip off his tunic or mantle, for all exercises were done naked, so that the master could see how the boy's body needed to be developed for health and beauty. Exercises were graded and fitted to the needs of each boy and the paidotribes was trained to be scientific as a *physiotherapist* is today. He carried a long forked stick as his sign of office, like the branch which umpires at the Games held in their hands. On the opposite page is a picture painted on a vase of two boys learning to wrestle in the palaestra (the Greek word for wrestling is 'pale'). You can see the paidotribes in the middle and on the right a boy with a pickaxe is preparing the ground for other wrestlers. What is hanging on the wall? Most of the exercises were performed to the sound of flutes.

Every village and town in Attica had its own small palaestra. Besides these, in Athens itself there were three big public sports

A wrestling lesson

grounds for physical education, open to boys and men, and there were no fees to pay. These were the gymnasia belonging to the city and free to all citizens. One of these was called the Akademeia (our word academy comes from it); it was outside the city wall of Athens to the east, by the river Eridanus. It was laid out with shady walks under the plane trees as well as a running track, jumping pit, parade ground and palaestra. Athenian men and boys walked to the Akademeia to practise athletics and to train for the Games. If you turn back to Chapter 1 you will find there a description of the athletic events which would be practised in the gymnasium. First the athletes rubbed themselves with oil to make their bodies supple and then powdered them with sand or a special yellow earth to close the pores and keep the body cool in the hot sun. After exercise they used a scraper called a *strigil* for removing the sweat and dust together. Many would finally have a shower bath or a swim in the river, especially before a dinner party.

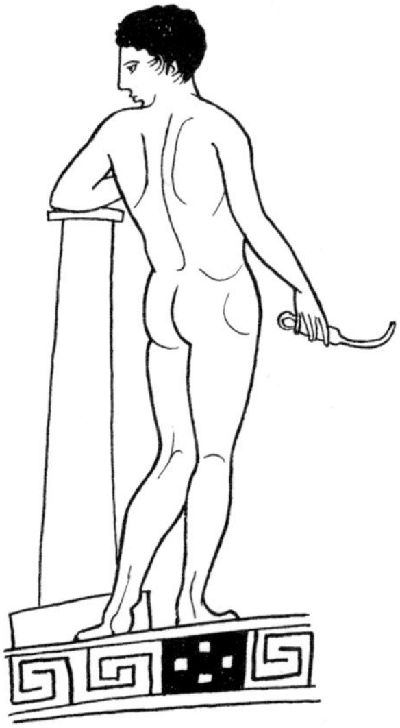

An athlete using a scraper

Athletes having a shower

Above is a picture painted on a vase showing athletes having a shower. The gymnasium was not used only for physical education. It was a favourite place also for discussion and for wandering teachers to give lectures.

Boys left their primary school at about fourteen years old, but those who need not earn their living because their parents were wealthy continued their education with these lectures in houses or the gymnasia for four more years, until they had to do their military training and service to the State. There were one or two secondary schools in Athens, but boys or their parents chose for themselves what subjects they would study. Mathematics, astronomy and rhetoric (public speaking) were very popular.

When he was eighteen years old, the young Athenian partly came of age. First of all, his *deme* or parish had to examine him to see if he was of true Athenian parentage and the correct age. Then he had to take a solemn oath saying:

> 'I will not disgrace my sacred weapons nor desert the comrade who is placed by my side. I will fight for things holy and things *profane*, whether I am alone or with others. I will hand on my fatherland greater and better than I found it. I will hearken to the magistrates and obey the existing laws and those hereafter established by the people. I will not consent unto any that destroys or disobeys the constitution, but will prevent him, whether I am alone or with others. I will honour the temples and the religion which my forefathers established. So help me Aglauros, Enualios, Ares, Zeus, Thallo, Auxo, Hegemone.' (These were all gods.)

After this he was called an *ephebos* and had to start his military training under the strict control of a special officer appointed by the State to take charge of all the epheboi for that year. He bought the rations for the mess and arranged the gymnastic training and taught drill on the parade ground. All the richer epheboi were expected to be cavalrymen and had to provide their own horses. Do you remember how they took part in the great procession at the Panathenaic festival?

At the end of their first year of training the epheboi all appeared in the open air theatre at the great spring festival in honour of Dionysus and gave a display. After the review, each one received a spear and shield from the State, or, if his father had been killed fighting for Athens, then the son received a complete outfit of armour. This was a kind of 'passing out' parade. The next year was spent in garrison duty and patrol work on the frontiers of Attica. Companies were moved about regularly so that they gained a thorough knowledge of their own country and were better able to defend it. The recruits finished their training at the age of twenty and became full Athenian citizens who might be called upon at any moment to do military service for their city state.

The Athenians were full of curiosity about everything under the sun and whenever a new teacher of wisdom came to Athens many flocked to hear him, especially the young men. The Greek word for wisdom is *sophia*, so these wandering teachers were nicknamed Sophists. Here is a story from the dialogue called Protagoras in which a young man named Hippocrates is so eager to learn from the famous teacher of wisdom Protagoras that he wakes up Socrates before dawn to ask if he will introduce him to Protagoras. The story is told by Socrates and shows how he liked to question young men and make them think for themselves.

> 'Last night, a little before daybreak, Hippocrates knocked violently on my door with his stick, and when it was opened, came straight in in a great hurry and shouted out: "Socrates, are you awake or asleep?"
>
> I recognised his voice and said: "That will be Hippocrates. No bad news I hope?"
>
> "Nothing but good," he replied.
>
> "I'm glad to hear it," said I, "what is it then, and what brings you here at such an hour?"
>
> Protagoras has arrived," he said, taking his stand beside me.
>
> "The day before yesterday. Have you only just found out?"
>
> "Only last evening," As he said this he felt for the bed and sat by my feet, adding: "Yes, yesterday evening, when I got back late from Oenoe. My slave Satyrus had run away from me. I meant to let you know that I was going after him, but something put it out of my head. When I got back and we had had dinner and were just going to bed, my brother mentioned to me that Protagoras had come. Late

as it was, I nearly came to see you straight away, then I decided it was really too far into the night; but as soon as I had slept off my tiredness, I got up at once and came here as you see."

I recognised his determination and the state of excitement he was in, and asked him: "What is your concern in this? Has Protagoras done you any harm?"

"Of course he has, Socrates," replied Hippocrates laughing. "He keeps his wisdom to himself instead of sharing it with me."

"Not at all," said I, "if you pay him sufficient to persuade him, he will make you wise too,"

"If it were only a question of that," he said despairingly, "I shouldn't keep back a penny of my own money, or my friends' money either. But this is just the reason why I have come to you, to persuade you to speak to him on my behalf. For one thing I am too young, and for another I have never seen nor heard Protagoras. Last time he came to Athens I was still a child. But you know, Socrates, everyone is singing his praises and saying that he is the cleverest of speakers. Do let's pay him a visit at once, to make sure of finding him in. He is staying, so I am told, with Callias. Come on."

"My dear Hippocrates," I said, "we can't go there at this early hour. Let's come out here into the courtyard and walk around it to pass the time until it gets light. Then we can go. Protagoras spends most of his time indoors, so don't worry; we are pretty sure to catch him there."

'So then we got up and walked about in the courtyard, and to try Hippocrates' metal I began to examine and question him. "Tell me, Hippocrates," I said, "it is your present intention to go to Protagoras and pay him money as a fee on your behalf. Now who do you think you are going to and what will he make of you? Suppose for instance you had it in mind to go to your namesake

Hippocrates of Kos, the doctor, and pay him a fee on your own behalf, and someone asked you in what capacity you thought of Hippocrates with the intention of paying him, what would you answer?"

"I should say, in his capacity as a doctor."

"And what would you hope to become?"

"A doctor."

"And suppose your idea was to go to Polyclitus of Argos or Phidias of Athens and pay them fees for your own benefit, and someone asked you in what capacity you thought of paying this money to them, what would you answer?"

"I should say, in their capacity as sculptors."

"To make you what?"

"A sculptor, obviously."

"Right," said I. "Now here are you and I going to Protagoras prepared to pay him money as a fee for you—our own if it is enough to satisfy him, or if not, our friends' resources thrown in as well. If then, seeing us so full of enthusiasm, someone should ask: 'Tell me, Socrates and Hippocrates, what do you suppose Protagoras is, that you intend to pay him money?', What should we answer him? What particular name do we hear attached to Protagoras in the sort of way that Phidias is called a sculptor and Homer a poet?"

"Well—Sophist, I suppose, Socrates, is the name generally given to him."

"Then it is as a Sophist that we will go to him and pay him?"

"Yes."

' "And if you had to face the further question, 'What do you yourself hope to become by your association with Protagoras?' "

'He blushed at this—there was already a streak of daylight to betray him—and replied: "If this is like the other cases, I must say 'To become a Sophist'."

"But wouldn't a man like you be ashamed", said I, "to face your fellow countrymen as a Sophist?"

* * * * *

'When we arrived at the doorway, we stopped to discuss a question which had arisen between us on the way and which we wished to bring to a satisfactory conclusion before entering the house. Accordingly we stood talking at the entrance till we had settled the matter. Now the porter must, I imagine, have overheard us; and I am inclined to think that, on account of the multitude of Sophist callers, he feels disgust with all who come to the house. At any rate, when we had knocked at the door and he had opened it and caught sight of us, "Bah," he cried out, "More Sophists, I declare, my master is engaged." At the same time, with both his hands, he slammed the door in our faces, with all the will in the world. So we knocked again; but our friend, without opening, called out, "Sirs, have you not heard that my master is engaged?"

"But, good porter," I urged, "we are neither come to call upon Callias, nor are we Sophists; so cheer up. It is Protagoras we want to see—take in our names." At length, with the greatest difficulty, we prevailed on the fellow to open the door to us.

'When we were inside we came upon Protagoras walking in the portico, and walking with him in a long line were, on one side Callias son of Hipponicus, his step-brother Paralus the son of Pericles, and Charmides son of Glaukon, and on the other side Pericles' other son Xanthippus, Philippides son of Philomelus, and Antimoerus of Mende, the most eminent of Protagoras's pupils, who is studying professionally, to become a Sophist. Those who followed behind listening to their conversation seemed to

> be for the most part foreigners—Protagoras draws them from every city that he passes through, charming them with his voice like Orpheus, and they follow spellbound—but there were some Athenians in the band as well. As I looked at the party I was delighted to notice what special care they took never to get in front or to be in Protagoras's way. When he and those with him turned round, the listeners divided this way and that in perfect order, and executing a circular movement took their places each time in the rear. It was beautiful.
>
> '"Next after him my eyes observed", as Homer says, Hippias of Elis sitting on a seat of honour in the opposite portico; and around him were seated on benches Eryximachus son of Acumenos and Phaedrus of Myrrhinex and Andron son of Adrotion, with some fellow citizens of his and other foreigners. They appeared to be asking him questions on natural science, particularly astronomy, while he sitting aloft on his throne held forth on their problems.'

Here you see how eager the young Athenians were to ask questions and learn something new—so eager that they would even get up at dawn and learn walking up and down with the great Sophist teacher. But Socrates' conversation with Hippocrates on the way shows us that many people disliked the Sophists. They thought they were just clever talkers and not really wise at all. It was the older men who were most suspicious of these wandering teachers, because they thought that the new teaching encouraged young men to be disrespectful to the gods and their parents and to ask too many questions. One night a terrible thing happened in Athens. Someone went out into the streets and damaged a lot of the statues of the god Hermes which guarded the doorways of many homes in the city. In the morning when this was found out, the people were very alarmed and shocked, for they believed that this would bring the city bad luck. The citizens could not find out who had done such a wicked thing, but they blamed the Sophists and the wild young man Alcibiades and his friends.

Do you remember how Alcibiades burst into Agathon's feast when Socrates was there? These two, Alcibiades and Socrates, were great friends, but they were as different as they could be. Alcibiades was extremely handsome, young and dashing, with plenty of money; he loved to make a great splash with it and be the centre of everything. In the first chapter we met him entering seven chariots at the Olympic Games and winning the race; afterwards he gave a grand banquet. He was the darling of Athens. Socrates, on the other hand, was an ugly, snub-nosed little man with no money; he never wanted to be praised and admired like Alcibiades, but he was a great thinker who asked a lot of deep questions. Many of the young men of Athens, besides Alcibiades, were fascinated by Socrates because he was such an unusual person. They followed him about and listened to him with great respect, especially one fair-haired young wrestler whose nick-name was Plato, which means broad-shouldered. Later he became a famous teacher himself and wrote down a great deal of the teaching of Socrates as dialogues between the teacher and his pupils.

Postscript

There is a sad ending to the story of Socrates. After the war against Sparta, which you will read about later in this book, the enemies of Socrates accused him of encouraging young men to be disrespectful to the gods and of being a dangerous person to have in Athens. They thought the gods were angry and that Socrates had brought the city bad luck. He was put on trial and condemned to death. His friends tried to persuade him to escape from the prison, but he refused, saying that he had lived under Athenian law and now was content to die under it. Plato wrote three dialogues about the last days of

Socrates whom he loved and admired so much. This is the story of his last hours in the prison, told in a dialogue between Phaedo who was there and a friend from another place.

ECHECRATES: Were you there with Socrates yourself, Phaedo, when was he executed?

PHAEDO: I was there myself.

ECHECRATES: Then what did the Master say before he died and how did he meet his end? Which of the Master's companions were with him? Or did the authorities refuse to let them be there, so that he passed away without a friend at his side?

PHAEDO: Oh no; some of them were there—quite a number in fact. I will try to describe it to you. Nothing gives me more pleasure than remembering Socrates, either by talking myself or by listening to someone else. My own feelings at the time were quite extraordinary. It never occurred to me to feel sorry for him, as you might have expected me to feel at the deathbed of a very dear friend. The Master seemed quite happy; he met his death so fearlessly and nobly. I could not help feeling that even on his way to the other world he would be under the care of God and that when he arrived there all would be well with him. So I felt no sorrow at all; at the same time I felt no pleasure when as usual we started a discussion. I felt a curious mixture of pleasure and pain combined, as I realised that in a little while my friend was going to die. All of us who were there felt much the same way, between laughing and crying.

Then Phaedo tells about the long discussion which they had with Socrates. At the end of it Socrates says:

"There is one way in which a man can be free from all anxiety about the fate of his soul: if in life he has given up bodily pleasures and has devoted himself to the pleasures of getting knowledge and so by decking his soul, not with a borrowed beauty but with its own, with self-control and goodness and courage and truth, has fitted himself to await his journey to the next world. You will each make this journey some day in the future, but for me the hour calls even now. In other words it is about time I took my bath."

* * * * *

'It was now nearly sunset. Socrates came and sat down, fresh from the bath. The prison officer came in and walked up to him. "Socrates," he said "I have come to know that you are the noblest and the gentlest and the bravest of all the men who have ever come here and now I am sure that you are not angry with me. So now—you know what I have come to say—goodbye, and try to bear what must be as easily as you can." As he spoke he burst into tears and went away. Socrates said: "Goodbye to you too; we will do as you say. Come, someone had better bring in the poison, if it is ready prepared."

"But surely, Socrates, the sun has not gone down yet. In other cases people have dinner and enjoy their wine long after they receive the warning and only drink the poison quite late at night. No need to hurry; there is plenty of time."

Socrates replied: "I shall gain nothing by drinking the poison a little later—I should only make myself ridiculous in my own eyes if I clung to life and hugged it when it has no more to offer. Come, do as I say." Crito's servant went out and came back with the man who carried the poison in a cup. When Socrates saw him he said: "Well, my good fellow, what ought I to do?"

"Just drink it," he said "and then walk about until you feel a weight in your legs and then lie down. Then it will act of its own accord." As he spoke he handed the cup to

Socrates who received it quite cheerfully. Socrates said: "I suppose I am allowed, or rather bound, to pray the gods that my removal from this world to the other may be prosperous. This is my prayer." With these words, quite calmly and without any sign of distaste, he drank the cup in one breath.

'Up till this time most of us had been fairly successful in keeping back our tears; but when we saw that he had actually drunk it, we could do so no longer. I covered my face and wept broken-heartedly—not for him, but for my own calamity in losing such a friend. Everyone in the room broke down, except Socrates himself who said: "Really, my friends what a way to behave! I am told that one should make one's end in a tranquil frame of mind. Calm yourselves and try to be brave." This made us feel ashamed and we controlled our tears.

'Socrates walked about and presently, saying that his legs were heavy, lay down on his back . . . (very soon after this he was dead).

'Such, Echecrates, was the end of our comrade, who was, we may fairly say, of all those whom we knew in our time, the bravest and also the wisest and the most upright man.'

6 People at Work in Athens

The busy town centre of Athens was called the Agora; it was north-west of the Acropolis and is marked on the plan on page 22. Just as the town centre of Plymouth was rebuilt after the Second World War, so in Athens after the Persian War Pericles and Phidias made new plans for the Agora. On the west side nearest the city wall was the Hill of Kolonus. On the top of this they built a temple of Hephaestus, the god of the smithy. Around the hill lived most of the metal workers, near their patron god; they made swords and shields and other weapons as well as bronze pots and pans for the home. At the foot of this hill was a row of public buildings. One was a new council chamber and dining hall for the councillors. Another was a round building for housing the official weights and measures; near this was the army headquarters. On the south

Temple of Hephaestus

A shoemaker's workshop, painted on a jar

side of the Agora were the law courts and also the mint where the silver coins were made. On three sides of the town centre there were long covered colonnades where people could walk and also do their shopping, for some of these colonnades had little shops, such as shoemakers and saddlers and wine sellers.

Every morning there was a busy market in the Agora. Stalls were set up soon after sunrise, as they still are on market days in some English towns today, and the country people tramped into the city as soon as the gates were open, bringing their vegetables or fruit or wine to sell to the townsfolk. The market was arranged in streets, with all the flower-sellers together and all the bread stalls in another part. These were kept by poor women, and apparently they had the same reputation as the fishwives of Billingsgate in London for swearing and bad language. The fishmongers were also noisy fellows who tried to charge high prices. The Athenians were very fond of fish and when a new catch arrived from the Piraeus harbour, they rang a bell in the market and everyone rushed to buy the best bargains, leaving everything else. An amusing story is told of a musician giving a recital on the harp in a room near the market, when suddenly the fish bell rang. Up started all his friends and left the room, except for one rather deaf old man. The musician came to him and said 'Thank you, Sir, for being the only man to have the manners to stay when the fish bell rang.' 'What,' said he, 'did you say it was the fish bell? Thanks. Goodbye,' and off he went.

The market finished at noon by the sun and the stalls were cleared away, but the Agora was still a busy place all through the day. Here men walked and talked under the colonnades, protected from the hot sun. There were plane trees, too, planted for shade, and at two corners there were fountains playing; one had nine spouts. So even in the hot and dusty afternoons you would often find little groups of men discussing and arguing in the Agora, sitting under the trees or the colonnades.

Another favourite place for picking up the latest gossip and discussing the news was the barber's shop. Athenian men were very particular about their hair and many of them had beards too, as you can see in the picture on page 77, but, as you read earlier in the book, there were no ladies' hairdressers as they did their own at home. The barber's shops were all together near the market place, just as the metal workers had their own part of the town, and also the potters. Most of these little shops were kept by foreigners as Athenian citizens did not think it was gentlemanly to keep a shop; a gentleman should own a piece of land.

Picking olives

Most Athenian citizens owned some land in Attica even though they lived in the city; no one who was not a citizen was allowed to own land. Many citizens were small farmers in Attica: the soil was poor, but vines and olives grew well and as you know already these were very important crops. The smallholders just managed to feed their families, but some citizens were large landowners like Pericles. He did not manage his estates himself, but employed a clever slave as his steward or bailiff to do this for him; all the produce from his land was brought into Athens and sold, and then the food for his household was bought in the market, because he did not want to spend time and energy on managing his estate. He was much more interested in making Athens a great and beautiful city than in making or saving money. This was true of many Athenian citizens; they would much rather be poor, or at any rate live quite simply and have time to listen to Socrates or the Sophist teachers, than give all their time to working hard and making money. They thought it was vulgar to aim at making money and rather despised people who paraded their wealth. Socrates was a very poor man, but this did not worry him; indeed, he wore no shoes and often went without food, yet hardly noticed this at all. He would never take any fee for his teaching. He was probably a stone-cutter, but did not spend much of his time working at his craft, which annoyed his wife very much.

Makers of statues were busy. Phidias and later Praxiteles were the most famous, but there were many others, because so many statues had to be made. Athens was full of them. Nearly every house had a statue of the god Hermes at its front door; there was one whole street where only makers of statues of Hermes lived. Often the sculptors would go to the palaestra to make sketches of athletes for their statues and any very handsome and well-proportioned young man might be asked to pose as a model for a statue of the god Apollo.

Stone-masons were naturally in great demand at Athens during Pericles' big building programme. The heavy work in the marble quarries at Mt Pentelikos was done by slaves, who, unlike the house slaves, had a miserable life. Then the big

Head of Apollo

blocks of marble had to be hauled into the city to be finished. You may wonder how this was done without any machines like cranes or lorries. We get the answer from an *inscription*. First of all they made a road from the quarry to the city, which had to be paved with grooved stones. Think for yourself what the grooves were for. The road which the Athenians made on the slopes of Mt Pentelicos can still be seen, with its grooves and at intervals some great blocks of marble which were left halfway, perhaps because they were faulty or damaged. Next they had to make waggons heavy and strong enough to bear the weight of the blocks of stone and then pairs of oxen were needed to drag the waggon. In this inscription it says that thirty to forty pairs of oxen were needed to move a single block and it took three days to drag it thirty miles! Each pair of oxen cost 4 *drachmas* and ½ *obol* per day. Just think now what an enormous amount of hard work and time and money it took to bring all those blocks of marble into Athens and up to the top of the Acropolis for the building of the Parthenon. No wonder they had a great festival of rejoicing when it was finished! In this work the free citizens of Athens joined willingly for the love of their city and their goddess. Their wages, paid by the state for this work, out of the Treasury of the Delian League, were 1 drachma a day. Some of the stonemasons who helped to build the temple called the Erechtheum were not citizens but foreigners and slaves, but they all seem to have worked together and received the same wage. An inscription says that each column was fluted by four to six masons working under a master mason, but the foreman and architect received the same wages as the labourers. (What would our trade unions think of that?).

There were no big factories or works in Athens, but there was one industry which was very important. This was the pottery industry or, as the Greeks called it, *kerameikos*. There was a special part of the city of Athens where all the potters lived and worked; you will find it marked on the plan of the city on page 22. Part was inside the walls and part outside the Dipylon Gate. Most of the potters were foreigners who had come to live and work at Athens and were called *metics*. They had to pay taxes and be registered, but could not vote or hold office: in other words, they were not citizens.

The potters made all shapes and sizes of jars, jugs and bowls and, as you know from many of the pictures in this book, they decorated them with patterns and figures. The potter's clay found in Attica turns a bright orange-red colour when it is fired in a well-ventilated kiln; this is called *terra-cotta*, which means baked earth. Before Pericles' time Athenian pots were decorated with black patterns and figures and so are called black-figure pots or vases (though remember they were for use as well as ornament). The pottery made in Pericles' days is covered with a brilliant glossy black sheen and the patterns and pictures are terra-cotta colour. This has puzzled modern potters for a long time as the black is not a glaze nor a varnish. Now a scholar has found out by experimenting that this shiny black colour is produced by painting with a red *slip* and then firing it in a special way so that the painted part becomes black in the firing. (If you are interested in the chemistry of pottery you can find out more about this process with the help of your teacher.) Athenian pots were fashionable in many Mediterranean towns and Athens had a big export trade in pottery.

The Athenians were great sailors like all the Ionian Greeks. They sailed their little ships between the thousands of islands and northwards away through the dangerous narrows of the Hellespont to the Black Sea; they told all sorts of travellers' tales about these far away lands. One tells of a golden fleece guarded by a great serpent and another of the warlike moon-maidens called the Amazons. Homer told how Odysseus had all kinds of adventures at sea on his way home from Troy; he just escaped being dashed to pieces between the clashing rocks of the Hellespont. But the Greek sailors discovered also that there was very good land for growing corn by the Black Sea and so, long ago, they had settled there as colonists. In the time of Pericles the townsfolk of Athens could not grow enough corn for themselves and so corn ships came regularly from the Black Sea bringing extra food for Athens.

Other merchant ships sailed to Egypt carrying a cargo of pottery and brought back perfumes or ivory. They sailed westwards, too, hugging the shore and islands most of the time

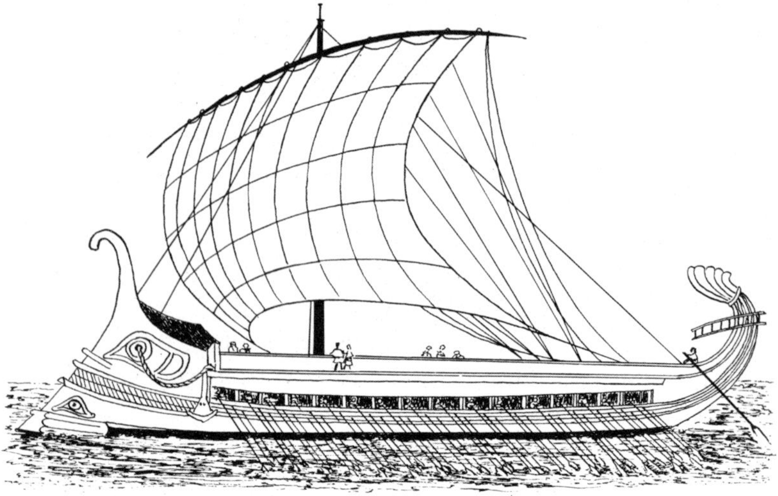

Greek trireme

and calling at the Greek cities of Sicily and Italy, up to Marseilles and along the coast of Spain as far as the 'Pillars of Hercules', which was their name for the Straits of Gibraltar. Everywhere the Athenians sailed they found Greek colonies where the people spoke their language and so they could trade easily. Sometimes new colonies were started, like the one at Thurii in Southern Italy; Herodotus, the historian, left Athens to go and live there. The fame of Athens was spread round the shores of the Mediterranean by these merchant sailors, so that even the names of famous writers of plays were known far and wide. It is said that at Syracuse some Athenian prisoners of war actually gained their freedom because they were able to repeat some lines from the latest play by the poet Euripides (whom you will read about in the next chapter).

Besides these merchant ships there were the ships of the Athenian Navy in the harbours at Piraeus. These were called *triremes* and they were propelled by oars, but also had sails which could be used in a fair wind. In a battle the sails were furled and the rowers had all the work to do. At the bows, just beneath the water level, there was a sharp timber beak, shod with iron or bronze, for ramming the enemy ships. Athens had a large navy and so many rowers were needed that some of them were metics or slaves, but citizens had to row, too, as part of their military service when required. The poorest citizens were the ordinary sailors for they were glad to have the wages. Sometimes the sailor citizens played quite a big part in settling the future plans for their city; because they wanted to be employed and paid by the city they voted for a naval expedition or a warlike policy rather than for peace.

The Athenians had no paper money. Nearly all their coins were made of silver and they were stamped with the owl of wisdom and the olive branch belonging to their goddess on one side and with Athene's head on the other. The smallest coin was half an obol. Six obols were equal to one drachma and the four drachma piece was called a stater. We cannot say exactly how much a drachma would be worth today, but it was the ordinary day's wage for a man.

Athenian coin

The silver for these coins was mined at Laurium by slaves. These were mostly prisoners of war and they were very badly treated, whereas the household slaves and those who worked in industry were well treated on the whole and often earned their freedom. Freed slaves became metics and could set up in business. Sometimes they became rich men, but they could not become full citizens of Athens, except by special decree of the Assembly.

7 Festivals

The Athenians enjoyed their religious festivals and there were a great many of them, for every god and goddess had a festival of his own; there were more than sixty festival days in the year. In July, which was the beginning of their year, came the festival of Athene, and every fourth year this lasted for six days. Everyone had a holiday. One day was given up to athletic competitions which included all the same events as the Olympic Games. Boys competed against boys, youths in another class, and men with men. The prizes were decorated vases full of olive oil, because Athene was the goddess who gave the olive to Athens. Each of the ten tribes chose twenty-four of their finest young men, and a prize was given for the best set; this was called the prize for fine manhood. Horse racing and chariot racing were included in the Panathenaic Games too.

A prize jar given at the Panathenaic Festival

On another day there were competitions in music and recitation of Homer's poetry. These were held in the new Hall of Song, called the Odeion, which Pericles had built on the south-east slope of the Acropolis. It was made of wood and had a special tent-shaped roof as a good sounding board. Competitors had to sing and accompany themselves on the harp or the lyre or the flute.

The festival was kept up at night too, with singing and dancing and torch races. These were relay races in which one chain of runners competed against another chain, handing a blazing torch along the line without letting it go out. Then came the greatest day of all when the whole city turned out for the procession escorting the gorgeous new robe for the statue of the goddess. This was the biggest and most splendid procession of all and you can read again the description of it on page 27. The Festival of Athene ended with a great feast and a regatta in the Piraeus harbour, with all kinds of side-shows.

Another important festival was the one held for five days in March to celebrate the coming of Spring. This was to honour the young god, Dionysus, who gave the vine to Attica and made the land fruitful. His festival was the time for dancing especially and the circular dancing floor with an altar in the middle was called an *orchestra*. (Notice how the word orchestra has changed its meaning in our day.) There had been an orchestra in the market place in the past and the audience stood round to watch the chorus singing and dancing. The musicians sat near the altar of Dionysus in the middle of the orchestra. Then an actor was introduced who spoke and was answered by the chorus and thus the drama or play began. Now a special place was needed for the audience, so that everyone could see and hear and this was called a theatre. It was made out of the southern slope of the Acropolis facing the sun, with seats cut into the hillside in tiers. In the centre of the front row sat the priest of Dionysus. Opposite him, on the further side of the orchestra, was a long low building rather like a temple, called the *skene*, in which properties were kept. If you look at the picture on page 79 you can see what the theatre at Athens looked like in the time of Pericles. This one at Epidauros has not been altered since it was made; the ruins of the skene are on the right and in front of it is a very small

Seat for the priest of Dionysus

stage. Today this open air theatre at Epidauros and the one at Athens too are still used for plays which were written and acted in the days of Pericles and the audience can hear every word, although the theatres hold up to 20,000 people. As the theatre was so large the actors wore masks and high boots and padded costumes. They had to speak very clearly and effectively so as to be heard and this was most important, for the plays were all written in poetry.

Some time before the great spring festival when plays were acted, the writers of plays gave their manuscripts to a committee, who chose three tragic or serious poets and five comic writers, for this was to be a competition for the best play. The duty and expense of training and equipping the chorus in each play was given to a wealthy citizen called a *choregus*. One chief actor, the *protagonist*, was allotted to each poet, so that the contest was fair, but one actor could play several parts and there were never more than three actors, all of them men.

On the first day of the festival all the citizens, men, women and boys, came streaming into the theatre at daybreak; the charge for admission was two obols, but a poor citizen could draw this from a special fund. Some carried cushions, for the seats were of stone and the plays lasted all day. Everyone wore a garland of ivy leaves and most people brought light refreshments. The front seats were for the judges (drawn by lot) and other officials, foreign envoys and victors in the games or other citizens who had brought honour to Athens. Special parts were reserved for the Council of Five Hundred, for the women and for the epheboi, the young men on military service. The audience was a very lively one and woe betide a poor actor who could not be heard or mispronounced a word; they would whistle and cluck their tongues and kick their heels and even pelt him with fruit or nuts! If the play was poor, they would 'throw it out', that is, drive it off the stage, but if it was a good strong play, well acted, then the audience was moved to feel fear and pity; they would weep for the hero's sufferings and be hushed to stillness before the doom of the gods. Sometimes, as a play reached its climax, they would sway to the rhythm of the poetry just as the chorus did.

A tragic actor

The whole morning was taken up by one set of tragedies, then the audience stretched their legs and had lunch and returned for the comedy (the funny play) in the afternoon, except the women; they went home, as the Athenians thought that the comedies were only suitable for men to see. For three days this went on and then the judges gave their verdict. The writer of the best tragedy and the writer of the best comedy received a prize of money, so did the best actor. The choregus who had provided the best chorus received a *tripod*, and he was usually so proud of it that he set it up on a pedestal in the street near the theatre called Tripod Street. For the rest of the year until the next festival came round the audience would be quoting lines from the tragedies and recalling the best jokes from the comedies.

Lysikrates' monument in Tripod Street

Head of Aeschylus

There were three great writers of tragedies whose plays have survived. First came Aeschylus, who fought at Marathon and Salamis for Greek freedom. He wrote a play about the struggle, called *The Persians*, showing how the great king Xerxes was punished by the gods for his pride. How the Athenians must have clapped and applauded this play! But it was a generous play in which Aeschylus showed pity for the defeated Persians as well as triumph in their downfall at Salamis. On page 96 you can read part of the speech which Aeschylus wrote for the messenger who has the terrible task of telling the Persian Queen Mother and all the Persians at home about the disaster at Salamis. In other plays Aeschylus used Homer's stories of the Trojan War for his plots. Sophocles, then a young man, danced at the victory celebrations after the defeat of Persia; he was a friend of Pericles and appointed by him to be chief treasurer for reorganising the Athenian empire; later he was a general. He wrote more than a hundred plays about the old heroes and won the prize many times. The third great poet was Euripides. He studied under the Sophist Protagoras whom we met before. One of Euripides' greatest plays, *Trojan Women,* is about the end of the great war between Greeks and Trojans. It shows vividly the misery of the captive women after the fall of Troy.

Unfortunately most of the comedies have been lost except those written by Aristophanes. He made fun of everyone and everything. In one play called *The Clouds* Socrates is suspended over the stage in a basket meditating; probably Socrates himself was sitting in the audience watching this play! In another Aristophanes makes fun even of Dionysus himself. In this play the god says that he is bored by his festival as there are no good poets nowadays; so he proposes to go down to the Underworld (Hades) and bring back to life one of the good old poets. He sets off with his slave, who grumbles at having to carry all the bundles. As it is a dangerous and difficult journey Dionysus dresses up in a lion's skin, imitating the mighty Heracles and calls on him for help; Heracles is convulsed with lasghter at the ridiculous sight of the god in his saffron robe and sandals with the lion skin draped on top. In fact, Dionysus is made to behave rather like Sir Andrew Aguecheek in Shakespeare's *Twelfth Night*, while the mighty Heracles is somewhat like Sir Toby Belch. Next the travellers have to cross the dark River Styx. The slave is told to walk, but the gruff old boatman, Charon, tells the god to get in and row. He protests, but there is nothing for it but to do as he is told and then the chorus of frogs starts croaking, making fun of Dionysus:

'Brekeke-kesh, koash, koash.'

Poor Dionysus gets a sore bottom and blisters, but at last reaches the Underworld. There he meets the dignified old poet, Aeschylus, and the 'clever rascal', Euripides. After a competition between the poets which includes weighing their verses in a huge pair of scales, the god decides that Aeschylus is the weightier poet after all and so takes him back to Athens.

These great plays, both comic and tragic, written by Athenian poets so long ago, are still acted today and, like Shakespeare's plays, they are translated into many languages. They belong to the whole world now.

The ancient theatre at Epidauros with a play in progress today

8 The Athenian Citizen Governing his City state

In the fifth century B.C. every Athenian citizen was expected to help govern his city state as well as to defend it, for Athens was governed by the people (*demos* in Greek). Our word 'democracy' comes from the Greek. Athens had not always been a democracy. Like other Greek city states she had had kings, warrior heroes like Theseus, noble families and also tyrants or, as we should call them, dictators. One of these called Hippias is mentioned by Herodotus as the friend and ally of the Persians (see page 13). He had been driven out of Athens in 510 B.C. by the nobles with Spartan help. One of the nobles was called Cleisthenes. He wanted to see Athens governed by all the people, not just by the nobles, so he managed, with the support of the townsfolk of Athens, to reform the government of Athens and to make it a democracy.

This is how his plan worked. Every citizen was registered in a deme or parish, as you read in chapter 5. There were many demes, some on the coast, some in the country of Attica, and some in Athens itself; the demes were grouped together to make up a tribe. There were ten tribes. The daily work of government was carried on by fifty councillors all drawn by lot from the citizens over thirty years of age in one tribe; they held office for one-tenth of a year, that is, for thirty-five or thirty-six days; then another fifty from another tribe took over, and they drew lots to decide which tribe it should be. They did not put the names into a hat, but into a machine. The councillors were paid a small daily wage and also received public dinners in the new council chamber near the Agora. These councillors from all the ten tribes made up the Council of Five Hundred. If any citizen wished to propose a new law

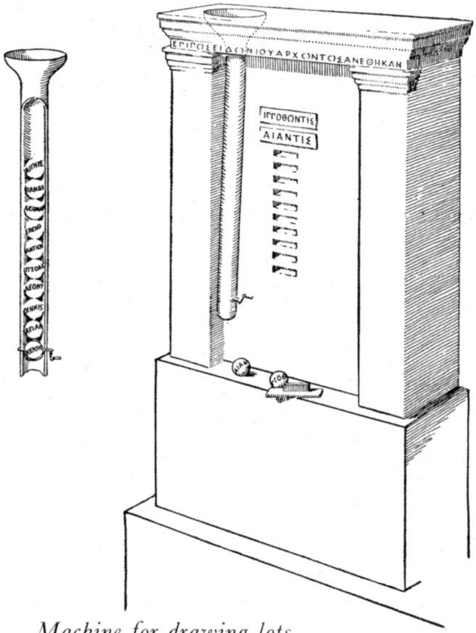

Machine for drawing lots

or bring up any business in the Assembly he had to take it first to the Council of Five Hundred. All the citizens rich and poor sat in the Assembly, which was called the *Ecclesia*. This met forty times in the year, that is, about every nine days, out of doors on the Pnyx Hill (this is marked on the plan of Athens on page 22). On a day when the Assembly had been called together, citizens who lived in the country or were out of the city looking after their farms, would have to get up soon after sunrise, put on a cloak and shoes and ride into Athens, or walk if they were too poor to own a horse. Others would have to come across the Strait from the Island of Salamis by boat. When they reached the Pnyx Hill, they sat down with their friends on the ground, facing the platform from which speeches were made. According to Aristophanes, the comic writer, the lazy townsfolk of Athens and Piraeus arrived later and latest of all the councillors came bustling up. As in our House of

Pnyx Hill

Commons the Assembly began with prayers. Many citizens did not bother to attend the Assembly, except when there was some very important business, such as making peace with Persia, or war against Sparta. Only when a decree had been proposed which affected one citizen, especially a proposal to banish him, did the constitution require six thousand citizens to be present. Banishment was a very popular punishment in Athens; if a general was unsuccessful and lost a battle he was likely to be banished. This was also a favourite weapon used by politicians against their enemies. Themistocles was banished for a time in spite of all he had done for Athens.

There were a great many magistrates and officials in Athens, and nearly all of them were chosen by lot. This was because the Athenians were always afraid that their officials or councillors would be bribed or bullied and so would favour the rich and powerful people. Do you know whether we have any laws in England about bribing government officials? In Athens nearly everyone, except the very poorest class who had little education, took some part in the government and every citizen was expected to know the laws. Do you remember that the boys learnt them by heart at school? People who broke the law, or had disputes to settle, were tried in the courts by jurymen; there was no judge specially trained in the law as we have. To prevent bribery they had very big juries and a complicated system of sorting out the jurymen so that no-one knew beforehand who would be trying a particular case. Under Pericles there were six hundred jurymen chosen by lot each year from each of the ten tribes, and he suggested that they should be paid two obols a day when they acted as jurymen.

The highest magistrates in Athens were the generals (*strategoi*). There were ten of them, one from each tribe, and each took command in turn, as you read in the story of the Battle of Marathon. Unlike the other magistrates, they were not paid, nor were they chosen by lot. They were elected annually by the whole Athenian people and could be re-elected year after year. You will easily see that it was plain common sense not to choose the generals by lot, but was it really sensible to elect them every year? Of course they could be re-elected, but suppose the people chose new generals each year, what would happen to the army?

I wonder what you think about the Athenian way of governing themselves as a whole? Do you think it is a good thing to have all the citizens discussing and settling everything? What happens if they are all carried away by bad, clever speeches and decide to do foolish things? Or change their minds very often? Or banish good people in a fit of temper? What happens if the councillors are ignorant or stupid men? Or if the jurymen are easily deceived by clever criminals? The Greeks themselves asked questions like this about government. Some thought that democracy was a bad kind of government and that all the governing should be done by the wisest men. But then they argued about how you found and educated the wisest men. On page 99 you can read some of Plato's ideas about bad and good government.

The Athenians criticised their own government and even allowed Aristophanes to make it look ridiculous, but they still believed deeply that all citizens should help to manage their own affairs. This really worked very well so long as the citizens were ready to take the advice of wise leaders. Themistocles, you remember, had been able to persuade them to make sensible plans for defending the city, and so had Pericles. He was elected general fifteen times and the people were willing to follow him. Because he was a nobleman (his mother was a niece of Cleisthenes) and owned a great deal of land, he did not have to earn his living. Instead he gave all his time and energy to serve Athens as general, both in war and in peace. He was a very cautious leader in war, but, after the great war against Persia, it was Pericles who inspired the Athenians to plan and build the lovely temples on the Acropolis. Now that the city was governed by the people, the nobles had to gain their support in the Assembly. This Pericles was able to do, because he was a very good speaker. Pericles was nicknamed The Olympian, probably because he was rather imposing and aloof in his behaviour. The sound of his voice was said to be like a musical instrument and for many years he was able to rule the people.

One reason for Pericles' popularity was that he tried to provide work for everyone by his big building schemes at home and by keeping up a strong navy abroad. But these had to be paid for and the only way was to use the tribute money paid by all the Greek states belonging to the Delian League. You will remember that the League had been started so that all the Greek states could help each other against enemies. The treasury was on the sacred island of Delos and the money in it was meant to be spent for the good of all the members. But Athens needed that tribute money and so the treasury was moved from Delos to Athens on the excuse that it would be safer from the Persians. Pericles argued that so long as the Athenian Navy protected the League members from Persians and pirates, the tribute money belonged to her, or rather to her goddess, and she could do what she liked with it. The allies thought this was most unfair; why should their money be used to make Athens beautiful? Pericles' enemies said that he was beautifying Athens 'as if it were some vain woman, decking herself out with costly stones and statues and temples worth millions of money'. The Athenians themselves began to treat their allies as though they were subjects; they interfered in the government of other cities, although they had promised not to do this and they sent their navy to punish islands which did not obey Athens. Of course this made all the other Greek city states very angry. Corinth and Sparta especially were always jealous of Athens, Corinth because Athens was stealing her trade and Sparta because Athens was becoming the leader of all Greece or Hellas in her place. So Corinth and Sparta stirred up all the trouble they could for Athens.

Head of Pericles

The people in these other Greek states were jealous and afraid of Athens. Feelings like this make people go to war. So in the year 431 B.C. a terrible war began between Athens and the other Greeks. This was the Peloponnesian War which dragged on for nearly thirty years and utterly ruined Athens. When the war started Pericles brought all the people of Attica into Athens, with their movable goods, and they camped between the Long Walls. Their enemies burnt the farms and crops and cut down the olive trees, but they could not provoke the Athenian hoplites to battle. Unfortunately, the overcrowding of the city caused an outbreak of plague and many people died. The Athenians thought that Apollo was angry with them, so they begged for peace, but Sparta refused to make peace. The Athenians then turned against Pericles saying that their misfortunes were all his fault and, in spite of all he could say in defence of his policy, the Assembly suspended him from office and fined him. Soon afterwards, they repented of this and elected him general again, but in 429 B.C. he died of plague.

After his death there was no one who could rule and lead the people wisely. Democracy only works well under good leaders and, particularly in wartime, bad leaders can bring disaster. Just when Athens most needed another great man, her Assembly began to listen too much to popular leaders who had little education and no knowledge of how to fight a war. All they could do was to shout in the Assembly and work up the people's feelings till they would agree to anything. The Greeks called this sort of leader a *demagogue* and the thoughtful citizens knew how dangerous he could be. But too many people in the Assembly were easily deceived and followed leaders like Cleon, the tanner, quite blindly.

Aristophanes tried to show them how stupid they were by making fun of these people in his plays. In one, called *The Knights*, Demos himself (by Demos, of course, Aristophanes means the people) is the chief character and the play shows how silly he could be. At the beginning he has two good slaves called Demosthenes and Nikias, who are really two Athenian generals, but now Demos is taken in by a cunning new slave, who is really the tanner, Cleon. He persuades Demos that his other two slaves are bad ones and so they are beaten. So Demosthenes, feeling very injured, welcomes the arrival of a new 'slave' or leader of the people, whose trade is making sausages.

DEMOSTHENES O happy man! celestial sausage seller!
Friend, guardian and protector of us all.
Come forward; save your friends and save the country.

SAUSAGE SELLER Do you call me?

DEMOSTHENES Yes, we called you to announce the high and happy destiny that awaits you. Set these poor wares aside and now bow down to the ground and adore the powers of earth and heaven.

SAUSAGE SELLER Heyday, why, what do you mean?

DEMOSTHENES O happy man!
Unconscious of your glorious destiny.
Now mean and unregarded; but tomorrow,
The mightiest of the mighty, Lord of Athens.

SAUSAGE SELLER Come, master, what's the use of making game?
Why can't ye let me wash the guts and tripe,
And sell my sausages in peace and quiet?

DEMOSTHENES O simple mortal cast those thoughts aside!
Bid guts and tripe farewell! Look there! Behold!
The mighty assembled multitude before ye
(Pointing to the audience)

SAUSAGE SELLER *(with a grumble of indifference)*: I see 'em.

DEMOSTHENES You shall be their lord and master,
The sovereign and the ruler of them all.
Of the assemblies and tribunals, fleets and armies;
You shall trample down the Senate underfoot,
Confound and crush the generals and commanders."

This is how Aristophanes makes fun of the people running after stupid and ignorant leaders; it is not surprising that they gave the people bad advice. They encouraged the Assembly to continue the war against Sparta, because they thought Athens and they themselves would grow richer and more powerful and the people would all receive wages from the State. Instead the war ruined Athens. It was Alcibiades who persuaded the Athenians to attack Syracuse, a very wealthy Greek city in Sicily; the Peace Party in Athens were defeated in the Assembly and a magnificent expedition set out, but it met with utter disaster and the whole expedition, the ships, the men and the weapons were all captured. Athens lost two hundred triremes, nearly all her navy. The prisoners were condemned to slavery in the stone quarries at Syracuse and suffered horribly. The General, Nikias, was captured and tortured to death. The Athenians were stunned when the news leaked through; they could not believe such a disaster could happen to Athens. Even after this the Athenians tried to continue the war, until they were finally starved into surrender to the Spartans in 404 B.C. Alcibiades had already deserted to the enemy. A Spartan garrison took possession of the Acropolis, the Long Walls were pulled down and the democratic government was abolished. Never again was Athens to be the political leader of Greece, yet her great experiment in government by the people under the law has inspired men and nations ever since to seek freedom and justice in government.

9 Athens, the School of Hellas

At the end of the first summer campaign of the Peloponnesian War, the bodies of those who had fallen in battle were brought to the cemetery, outside the Dipylon Gate of Athens, for burial. Both men and women mourners attended the state funeral and afterwards Pericles spoke to the people. His speech was remembered and recorded by his friend and admirer, Thucydides, who wrote a history of the Peloponnesian War, and this funeral oration is one of the most famous speeches ever made in the world's history, because it tells us of the ideals and achievements of a wonderful people. Here is a part of it:

'Our constitution is called a democracy, because it is in the hands of the many, not of the few. But while the law secures equal justice to all alike, talent is also recognised, and when a citizen is in any way distinguished, he is preferred for the public service, not as a matter of privilege, but on grounds of excellence alone. Neither is poverty a bar, but a man may benefit his country whatever be the obscurity of his condition. As we have given free play to all in our public life, so in our private intercourse we are not suspicious of one another, nor angry with our neighbour if he does what he likes; we put on no sour looks at him, which, though they leave no mark, are unpleasant. Open and friendly in our private intercourse we cherish a spirit of reverence in our public acts; we are kept from wrong by respect for authority and the laws, particularly those for the protection of the oppressed. We have not forgotten to provide our spirits with many relaxations from toil; there are regular games and festivals throughout the year; our home life is refined; and the delight we daily feel in all these blessings helps to banish sadness. Our city is equally admirable in peace and war; for we are lovers of the beautiful, yet simple in our tastes, and we cultivate the mind without loss of manliness. Wealth to us is not mere material for vain glory but an opportunity for achievement. With us to avow poverty is no disgrace; the true shame is in doing nothing to avoid it. If few of us are originators we are all sound judges of policy. In our opinion the great impediment to action is not deliberation, but the want of knowledge gained by discussion preparatory to action. For we have the peculiar power of thinking before we act and of acting too, whereas other men are courageous from ignorance but hesitate on reflection. In doing good we are unlike others, for we make our friends by conferring, not by receiving favours. We alone benefit our neighbours not upon calculation of interest, but in the confidence of freedom and in a frank and fearless spirit. In a word, I claim that Athens is the school of Hellas and that the individual Athenian in his own person clearly possesses the power of adapting himself to the most varied activities with the utmost versatility and grace.'

If you have read the book in this series on Alexander the Great, you will know that he loved and admired Athens and that his tutor was a very famous Athenian called Aristotle. Yet Alexander lived nearly a hundred years after Pericles made his great speech. The fine achievements of Athenians had lasted for a century and were still very much alive to this Macedonian king so that he tried to spread their ideas all over his empire. Many centuries later a great Roman writer called Plutarch wrote enthusiastically about the days of Pericles and the glory of Athens, which he saw for himself. This is what he says:

'So the buildings arose as imposing in their sheer size as they were *inimitable* in the grace of their outlines, since the artists strove to excell themselves in the beauty of their workmanship. And yet the most wonderful thing about them was the speed with which they were completed. Each one possessed a beauty which seemed venerable the moment it was born and at the same time a youthful vigour which makes them appear to this day as if they were newly built.'

Ever since Alexander's time, in fact, people of all ages and races have loved and admired Ancient Athens and the amazing achievements of her citizens. So Pericles could rightly claim that Athens was the school of Hellas, Athens the violet-crowned.

10 Further Readings from famous Greek writers

1. In the Iliad, Homer tells the story of the war between the Greeks and the Trojans. Achilleus was one of the Greek leaders, but he quarrelled with Agamemnon and refused to fight. He lent his armour to his friend Patroclos and in a fierce fight with Hector, the Trojan hero, Patroclos was killed and the famous armour was seized as booty. Achilleus grieved for his friend, but his mother, the goddess Thetis, was alarmed because he had no armour in which to fight. So she went to the lame god of the metal workers called Hephaistos and asked him to make new armour for her son. This he did and Homer here describes the making of a wonderful shield for Achilleus.

And the renowned smith of the strong arms made elaborate on it
a dancing floor, like that which once in the wide spaces of Knosos
Daidalos built for Ariadne of the lovely tresses.
And there were young men on it and young girls, sought for their beauty
with gifts of oxen, dancing, and holding hands at the wrist. These
wore, the maidens long light robes, but the men wore tunics
of finespun work and shining softly, touched with olive oil.
And the girls wore fair garlands on their heads, while the young men
carried golden knives that hung from sword-belts of silver.
At whiles on their understanding feet they would run very lightly,
as when a potter crouching makes trial of his wheel, holding

it close in his hands, to see if it will run smooth. At another
time they would form rows, and run, rows crossing each
other. And around the lovely chorus of dancers stood a great
multitude
happily watching, while among the dancers two acrobats
led the measures of song and dance revolving among them.
He made on it the great strength of the Ocean River
which ran around the uttermost rim of the shield's strong
structure.
Then after he had wrought this shield, which was huge
and heavy,
he wrought for him a corselet brighter than fire in its
shining,
and wrought him a helmet, massive and fitting close to his
temples,
lovely and intricate work, and laid a gold top-ridge along it,
and out of pliable tin wrought him leg-armour. Thereafter
when the renowned smith of the strong arms had finished
the armour
he lifted it and laid it before the mother of Achilleus.
And she like a hawk came sweeping down from the snows of
Olympos
and carried with her the shining armour, the gift of
Hephaistos.

From Homer's *Iliad*.

2. *Herodotus tells how three hundred Spartans bravely tried to hold back the whole of Xerxes' great army.*

[Xerxes reaches the narrow mountain pass of Thermopylae and sends a spy to see what the Greeks are doing. He reports that the Lacedaemonians (the Spartans) are doing gymnastics and combing their long hair. Xerxes laughs but the spy warns him that when the Spartans do their hair carefully, they mean to fight for their lives.]

'Xerxes waited four days, expecting the Greeks to run away. When, however, he found that on the fifth day they were not gone, thinking their firm stand was mere impudence, he grew angry and sent against them the Medes and Cissians with orders to take them alive and bring them into his presence. Then the Medes rushed forward and charged the Greeks, but fell in vast numbers. Others took the places of the slain, but suffered terrible losses. Then it became clear to the king that though he had plenty of combatants he had very few warriors.

'Then the Medes, having met so rough a reception, withdrew from the fight and their place was taken by the band of Persians whom the king called his 'Immortals'. Everyone thought they would soon finish the business, but they had no better success. The Lacedaemonians were far more skilful in fight than their adversaries, often turning their backs, pretending to run away, on which the barbarians would rush after them with much noise, when the Spartans would wheel round and face their pursuers, destroying vast numbers of the enemy. At last the Persians, finding that all their efforts to capture the pass failed, withdrew to their own camp. During these battles it is said that Xerxes, who was watching, three times leapt from his throne in terror for his army.

'Next day the combat was renewed but with no better success. The Greeks were so few that the barbarians hoped they were now disabled by wounds. But the Greeks were drawn up in detachments according to their cities and bore the brunt of the battle in turns. So when the Persians found no difference between that day and the preceding, they again retired to their camp.'

[Just when Xerxes was in despair, a traitor Greek, for the sake of a rich reward, came to tell the king that there was a secret path over the mountains by which he could get behind the Greeks. Xerxes was overjoyed and at once sent troops to climb stealthily over the top by night. The night was very still and the Phocians guarding the top of the mountain heard the rustling of leaves but were so amazed when they spotted the barbarian army that they fled. So the main Greek army guarding Thermopylae had very little warning that they were betrayed.]

'Then the Greeks held a council to consider what they should do: some were against quitting their post, others wanted to. So some went home; part, however, resolved to remain and to stand by Leonidas [the Spartan general] to the last. It is said that Leonidas himself sent away the troops who departed, but thought it unseemly that either he or his Spartans should quit the post which they had been especially sent to guard.

'So the barbarians under Xerxes began to draw nigh and the Greeks under Leonidas, as they now went forth determined to die, advanced much further than before until they reached the more open part of the pass. Previously they had fought at the point where the pass was narrowest. Now they joined battle beyond the defile and carried slaughter among the barbarians who fell in heaps. For the Greeks, reckless of their own safety and desperate, since they knew that, as the mountain had been crossed, their destruction was near, went with the most furious valour against the barbarians.

'By this time the spears of the greater number were all shivered and with their swords they hewed down the Persians, and here, as they strove, Leonidas fell fighting bravely.'

[Finally the Persians who had crossed the mountain attacked them from the rear.]

'The Greeks, informed that they drew near, changed their fighting. Drawing back into the narrowest part of the pass, they posted themselves on a hillock, where they stood all drawn up together in one close body. Here they defended themselves to the last, such as still had swords using them and the rest resisting with their teeth and hands till the barbarians who now encircled them upon every side, overwhelmed and buried the remnant which was left beneath showers of missiles. Thus nobly did the whole three hundred of the Lacedaemonians behave.'

From the *History* of Herodotus

3. *Aeschylus in his play* The Persians *makes a messenger announce to the Persian Queen Mother the news of the terrible naval defeat at Salamis.*

A Hellene from the Athenian army came and told
Your son Xerxes this tale: that, once the shades of night
Set in, the Hellenes would not stay, but leap on board,
And, by whatever secret route offered escape,
Row for their lives. When Xerxes heard this, with no thought
Of the man's guile, or of the jealousy of gods,
He sent this word to all his captains: 'When the sun
No longer flames to warm the earth and darkness holds
The court of heaven, range the main body of our fleet
Threefold to guard the outlets and the choppy straits.'
Then he sent other ships to row right round the isle,
Threatening that if the Hellene ships found a way through
To save themselves from death, he would cut off the head
Of every Persian captain.
Our crews then, in good order and obediently,
Were getting supper; then each oarsman looped his oar
To the smooth rowing-pin; and when the sun went down
And night came on, the rowers all embarked, and all
The heavy-armed soldiers; and from line to line they called
Cheering each other on, rowing and keeping course
As they were ordered. All night long the captains kept
Their whole force cruising to and fro across the strait.
Now night was fading; still the Hellenes showed no sign
Of trying to sail out unnoticed; till at last
Over the earth shone the white horses of the day,

Filling the air with beauty. Then from the Hellene ships
Rose like a song of joy the piercing battle-cry,
And from the island crags echoed an answering shout.
The Persians knew their error; fear gripped every man.
They were no fugitives who sang that terrifying
Paean, but Hellenes charging with courageous hearts
To battle. The loud trumpet flamed along their ranks.
At once their frothy oars moved with a single pulse,
Beating the salt waves to the bo'suns' chant; and soon
Their whole fleet hove clear into view; their right wing first,
In precise order, next their whole array came on,
And at that instant a great shout beat on our ears:
'Forward you sons of Hellas! Set your country free!
Set free your sons, your wives, tombs of your ancestors,
And temples of your gods. All is at stake: now fight!'
Then from our side in answer rose the manifold
Clamour of Persian voices; and the hour had come.
At once ship into ship battered its brazen beak.
A Hellene ship charged first and chopped off the whole stern
Of a Phoenician galley. Then charge followed charge
On every side. Soon in that narrow space
Our ships were jammed in hundreds; none could help another.
They rammed each other with their prows of bronze and some
Were stripped of every oar. Meanwhile the enemy
Came round us in a ring and charged. Our vessels heeled
Over; the sea was hidden, carpeted with wrecks
And dead men; all the shores and reefs were full of dead.
Then every ship we had broke rank and rowed for life.
The whole sea was one din of shrieks and dying groans,
Till night and darkness hid the scene. If I should speak
For ten days and ten nights, I could not tell you all
That day's agony. But know this: never before
In one day died so vast a company of men.

From *The Persians* by Aeschylus

4· *In his play* The Knights *Aristophanes shows how the middle classes, represented by knights with hobby horses, can turn against the popular political leader Cleon, the tanner.*

CHORUS OF KNIGHTS (*closing round Cleon*):

Close around him and confound him, the confounder of us all.
Pelt him, pummel him and mawl him; rummage, ransack, overhaul him
Overbear him and out-bawl him; bear him down and bring him under,
Rogue and villain! rogue and cheat! rogue and villain I repeat!
Spit upon him as you see; spurn and spit at him like me.

CLEON: Worthy veterans of the jury, you that either right or wrong
With my threepenny provision, I've maintained and cherished long,
Come to my aid! I'm here waylaid—assassinated and betrayed.

CHORUS: Rightly served! we serve you rightly, for your hungry love of wealth!
Him besides, the wealthy man, retired upon an easy rent,
Hating and avoiding party, noble-minded, indolent,
Fearful of official snares, intrigues and intricate affairs,
Him you mark; you fix and hook him, whilst he's gaping unawares;
Down you cast him, roast and baste him and devour him at your ease.

CLEON: Yes, assault, insult, abuse me! This is the return I find!

CHORUS: Out, away with him! the slave! the pompous empty, fawning knave!
Does he think with idle speeches to deceive and cheat us all?

Pelt him here and bang him there; and here and there and everywhere!

From *The Knights* by Aristophanes

Plato disapproves of Athenian democracy; it looks very fine because it seems to give everyone freedom, but when it leads to quarrelling and disorder—like the scene in The Knights—*it is a bad form of government. He writes about this in* The Republic.

'In the first place a democracy is free; and the State is full of freedom and frankness—a man may say and do what he likes. And where freedom is, the individual is clearly able to order for himself his own life as he pleases, so that in this kind of State there will be the greatest variety of human character. Apparently it is the most beautiful of all constitutions—like a coloured dress embroidered with every sort of flower. There are many men to whom this State, embroidered with every kind of character, will appear to be the most beautiful of States. There being no necessity for you to govern in this State, even if you have the capacity, or to be governed, unless you like, or to go to war when the rest go to war, or to be at peace when others are at peace, unless you so choose—is not this a way of life which for the moment is supremely delightful? Democracy is a charming form of government, full of variety and disorder, and dispensing a sort of equality to equals and unequals alike.'

[But there is one great thing wrong with democracy: everyone goes his own way and there is no unity. But unity matters a great deal to Plato.]

'Can there be a greater evil in a State than discord and distraction and plurality where unity ought to reign? Or any greater good than the bond of unity? There is unity where there is community of pleasures and pains—where all the citizens are glad or grieved on the same occasions; and where there is no common but only private feeling a State is disorganized—when one half of its people are delighted and the other half are plunged in grief at the same events happening. Such differences begin in a quarrel about 'mine' and 'thine', 'his' and 'not his', and the best-ordered State is that in which the greatest number of persons apply the words 'mine' and 'not mine' in the same way to the same thing.'

[Plato goes on to argue that to get this unity it is best to have a State in which you share your wives and all your property! He also thinks that it is better to be ruled by a special class of rulers educated for the job than by ignorant people.]

'Our rulers must be lovers of their country, tried by the test of pleasures and pains, and neither in hardships nor in dangers must they lose their patriotism—those who fail in the test must be rejected, but those who always emerge unstained, like gold tried in the fire, shall be made rulers and receive honours and rewards in life and after death. And do not suppose that there will be many of them; for the gifts which are necessary rarely grow together; they are mostly found in shreds and patches. When our rulers have reached the age of fifty, then let those who have won through and have excelled in every sort of action and knowledge be introduced at last to their final task: the time has now arrived when they must raise the eye of the soul to the universal light and behold the Absolute Good; for this is the pattern by which they must rule the State and the lives of people and their own lives too, toiling at politics and ruling for the public good.'

From Plato's *Republic*

How many of Plato's ideas do you agree with?

The Caryatids: carved figures on the south side of the Erechtheum on the Acropolis

THINGS TO DO

1. Collect Greek postage stamps and find out how many of the designs are based on objects or buildings of Athens in the fifth century B.C.
2. Make a list of all the ways in which olive oil was used in Ancient Athens.
3. Describe a wedding in Ancient Athens.
4. Paint a picture of either the Panathenaic Procession or the Olympic Games.
5. Find out how far Phidippides must have run from Athens to Sparta, remembering that he did not fly over the mountains. How long is the Marathon race today? How did it get its name?
6. Write a play about an Athenian boy and his family and his paidagogos.
7. Read some of the *Iliad* or the *Odyssey* in translation.
8. Make a list of all the English words you can think of which have come from Greek ones mentioned in this book, e.g. athletics from *athlos* meaning a contest.
9. Act a part of Aristophanes' play *The Frogs*.
10. Ask your best reader in class to read aloud the messenger's description of the Battle of Salamis on page 96. Try to borrow from your public library a translation of *The Persians* by Aeschylus and read some more speeches from it.
11. Discuss the Athenian plan for paying wages (see page 68). Do you think this was fair?
12. Democracy comes from *demos*. Can you think of any other words to do with government which might come from Greek words? Make a list and then check up with the dictionary to see if you are right.
13. Geography, geology and geophysics all come from Greek words. What does 'geo' mean?
14. Write a play about Socrates and act it.
15. Choose six proper names from this book, e.g. Themistocles, and using the alphabet on page 47, write them in the Ancient Greek letters. What I have written on page iv To the Reader will help you too.
16. Study some of the Greek vases in this book and then paint a design for either the border of a tunic or a girdle for an Athenian girl (or you could weave one).

17. Write a detailed diary for one day in the life of either a boy or girl aged about fourteen. Decide first whether the boy's or girl's

18. Hold a class discussion on the good and bad points of the Athenian kind of government (read again pages 80–88 and 99–100).
19. What is the Hippocratic Oath? Find out all you can about it.
20. Imagine you are a B.B.C. interviewer visiting Athens in the year 429 B.C., when the war against Sparta was going badly and plague had broken out in the crowded city. Write a report on what you see and hear.

GLOSSARY OF GREEK WORDS

Acropolis, fortified hill top
Athlos, contest
Caryatids, statue of girls used as pillars
Choregus, trainer of the Greek chorus
Deme, parish
Demos, the people
Diskos, disc
Drachma, an Athenian silver coin
Ecclesia, general assembly of people
Ephebos, young Athenian man (18–20)
Halteres, jumping weights
Hellanodikai, officials in charge of the Olympic Games
Hoplites, heavy-armed foot soldiers
Kerameikos, potteries
Metic, foreigner allowed to live and work in Athens but not to become a citizen.
Nike, Victory
Obol, small Athenian coin
Orchestra, circular dancing floor
Paidagogos, slave in charge of Athenian schoolboy
Paidotribes, gymnastics master
Palaestra, wrestling school
Pale, wrestling
Pankration, all-in wrestling
Parthenos, maiden
Pentathlon, five athletic contests
Pente, five
Peplos, robe
Skene, room in which theatre properties were kept.
Sophia, wisdom
Stade, about 200 yards
Stater, a large silver coin equal to 4 drachmas
Stoa, covered colonnade
Strategoi, generals (singular—strategos)
Strigil, scraper, used by athletes
Symposium, drinking together and holding a discussion

GLOSSARY

betrothal, the formal engagement between a boy and a girl.
brazier, movable basket for a fire.
constitution, form of government.
censer, metal container for burning incense used in temples and churches.
demagogue, popular leader without much experience or good sense.
demolish, to, to pull down.
dialect, variation of a language, e.g. Yorkshire has its own dialect of English.
dowry, money or goods given to a girl by her father when she marries.
frieze, long strip of painting or sculpture on a wall.
inimitable, cannot be imitated.
inscription, words which are carved or painted, usually on a wall, to record a special happening.
libation, wine or other liquid poured out to honour a god.
lyre, musical instrument with seven strings.
portico, porch.
protagonist, a person who leads or fights for a cause or for other people.
profane, the opposite of sacred.
oracles and Delphic Oracle, forecasts of events or advice given by priests or priestesses of a god or goddess—so the servant of the gods was also called the oracle. The most famous was at Delphi.
sanctuary, place sacred to a god.
scrutiny, careful look at people or things to see if they are keeping certain rules.
sesame, plant bearing seeds which contain edible oil.
slip, mixture of water and clay which is used for painting in making pottery.
stylus, pointed writing implement like a skewer.
terracotta, earth (*terra*) which is baked (*cotta*) in a kiln or in the sun and so becomes a pinkish orange colour.
tripod, metal ring standing on three legs.
trireme, ship with either three banks of oars or three men rowing each oar.
unique, the only one of its kind.
vessel, pot or container for any liquid.
writing tablet, flat square pad covered with wax for writing on with a stylus.

OTHER LONGMAN MATERIALS ON GREEK HISTORY

Then and There
Alexander the Great
Ancient Crete and Mycenae

Aspects of Greek Life
64pp illustrated topic books

The Greek Theatre
Greek Exploration and Seafaring
Mycenae
Greek Art and Architecture
Minoan Crete
Greek Athletics
Greek Everyday Life

Related Filmstrips

Then and There
The Ancient World
(4 strips)

Common Ground
Life in Ancient Greece